The Art Of
Sign Language

Christopher Brown

THUNDER BAY
P · R · E · S · S
San Diego, California

Thunder Bay Press
An imprint of the Baker & Taylor Publishing Group
THUNDER BAY 10350 Barnes Canyon Road, San Diego, CA 92121
P · R · E · S · S www.thunderbaybooks.com

Produced by Salamander Books,
an imprint of Anova Books Company Ltd.,
10 Southcombe Street, London W14 0RA, U.K.

© 2002 PRC Publishing Ltd.

All notations of errors or omissions should be addressed to Thunder Bay Press,
Editorial Department, at the above address. All other correspondence (author inquiries,
permissions) concerning the content of this book should be addressed to
Salamander Books, 10 Southcombe Street, London W14 0RA, U.K.

ISBN-13: 978-1-59223-057-0
ISBN-10: 1-59223-057-1

Library of Congress Cataloging-in-Publication Data
Brown, Christopher, 1954–
The art of sign language / Christopher Brown.
p. cm. Originally published: London: PRC Pub., 2002.
ISBN 1-59223-057-1
1. Signed English. 2. Sign language. I. Title.
HV2474.B77 2003
419.7--dc21   2003044023

Printed and bound in China by Toppan Leefung Printing Ltd.
14 15 16 17 18 15 14 13 12 11

ACKNOWLEDGMENTS:
The author would like to thank his assistant, John Clements, without whose help this
book would not have been possible. He would also like to thank the photographer,
Ian Parry, and Cheryl Thomas from Chrysalis Books for making the
photography shoot such a pleasurable experience.

PHOTO CREDITS: All photography by Ian Parry.

contents

Sign language is a useful and highly effective tool to facilitate ease of communication for those with hearing difficulties. In most of its forms, sign language has many similarities with its spoken counterpart, the most striking of which is that it too is a living language, which is constantly undergoing change and development.

On the North American continent, there are two distinctly different ways of using sign language, but both mainly share the same vocabulary. American Sign Language (A.S.L. in its abbreviated form) was originally developed to express whole thoughts or ideas. Although it does have a grammatical structure of sorts, this is very different from the syntax that we are accustomed to using when speaking English. However, having few grammatical rules to adhere to, it is usually the preferred way for two hearing impaired people to communicate between themselves.

Signed English (or S.E.) uses the signed vocabulary of A.S.L. but follows the word order, sentence structure and grammar that we are familiar with in spoken English. The philosophy behind the development of "Signed English" is simple and based upon the way any child would learn its first language. Apart from the use of a sign to express a word or a series of signs to express a sentence, the English words are spoken simultaneously and body language employed to express and emphasize any emotion or feeling.

An interesting statistic is that less than five percent of all hearing impaired children have two hearing impaired parents, so it is important that this form of sign language is used by children learning from scratch. They are then communicating in a slightly different way but using the same grammar and sentence structure as their other hearing family members and contemporaries. Apart from learning the important tool of communication by manual signs, it encourages them to develop other skills such as lip-reading, making their communication skills more diverse.

4

PREFACE

Signed English uses two types of signs within its construction, words and markers. We have already discussed the words and their relationship to A.S.L. It is the sign markers which are used for grammatical purposes and may indicate tense, a plural, or be used to turn a verb into a noun.

The most important tool used in a manual sign system is finger spelling. Each vowel and consonant is represented by a different shape on one hand. Although a little slower than using a sign for each word, finger spelling is always used to prevent ambiguities in names and addresses and whenever an obscure or new word is encountered for which there is not yet a recognized sign.

It must also be noted that despite the ease of travel and communication in the 21st century, most spoken languages retain regional differences, both in terms of vocabulary and colloquialism. This is also common to sign language, however it is often very interesting to research and discover why a particular sign has come to be used in one specific area.

When learning something new, it is important to make it an enjoyable experience. As a hearing person, when I started to learn sign language I was so lucky to have many positive experiences and to be encouraged in my quest for this knowledge by hearing impaired friends who made the whole process fun. Please be encouraged to use any knowledge of sign language you are able to gain, you will find it most rewarding and be encouraged to progress to a higher level.

This publication is intended to be used as a very basic guide to sign language for the complete novice. We have tried to keep things as simple as possible to enable anyone to use this book to help them in a situation where some sign language skills are required.

Although each sign represented bears a written explanation as to how to make the sign, this explanation is intended merely as a tool to compliment the photograph. Study the photograph first and then refer to the explanation should any clarification be necessary.

In order to make it possible to use this book as a point of reference at any time, we have minimized the use of written abbreviation, which, we hope, will not require a formal key. The only true abbreviation used is "R" for right and "L" for left.

Many publications dealing with sign language list hand shapes and continually refer to these throughout the publication. To avoid the reader constantly having to be aware of these shapes, and to get away from needing background knowledge, I have used the signs themselves rather than asking the reader to form his hand into a particular shape. (In the first section, however, I have explained these basic hand shapes purely for the reader's reference.) For example, the written explanation for the word "aunt" reads, "*R 'A' sign palm out, wiggle at side of R cheek.*" So the way to interpret this would be, *"Sign the letter A with the right hand with the right palm facing outward. Having formed the hand shape in this way, wiggle it at the side of the right cheek."*

Finger spelling

The most useful thing that anyone interested in sign language can learn is to finger spell. Obviously, sign languages have been developed to avoid the necessity of spelling every word, but in any emergency a finger spelled word can be of the greatest use. In fact, when using sign language, both

hearing and hearing impaired people cannot know every single sign, as they constantly change and evolve, so finger spelling will be used in many situations. The same applies to spoken English where we occasionally encounter a word we have not met previously. Finger spelling is always used for names, days of the week and months of the year. Although all names are finger spelled, the spelling may be executed in such a way as to emphasize an individual's visible characteristics and to personalize the spelling of the name.

Sentence structure

The sentence structure used in Signed English is exactly the same as the format, which we use in spoken English, enabling any sentence to be literally translated word for word.

Markers

However, just as with spoken English certain changes take place in Signed English when a part of speech becomes a different part of speech. For example, when the adjective "slow" (the *slow* train) becomes used as an adverb (the train goes *slowly)* in written and spoken English we show this change by the use of the "-ly" suffix.

In Signed English, the corresponding change is reflected by using a sign marker, which is shown in this book along with how to use them.

There is one other special marker called an agent/thing or agent/person marker. This is used to change a verb into a noun indicating the person or thing that fulfils that function. For example, the verbs "teach, speak, run, and sing" would be turned into the nouns "teacher, speaker, runner, and singer." This change is made by placing both palms inwards at chest level and slowly lowering them simultaneously along the line of the body.

7

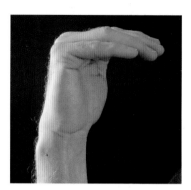

BENT

Fingers bent at knuckles and touching.

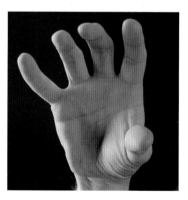

AND

All fingertips touching.

CLAWED

Splayed bent fingers.

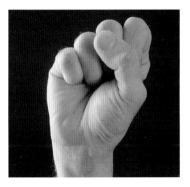

CLOSED
Fist shape.

CURVED
Fingers touching each other and hand curved.

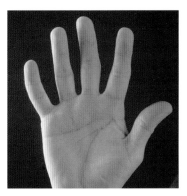

OPEN
Open flat hand with splayed fingers.

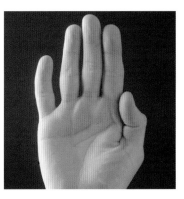

FLAT
Hand flat with fingers touching.

the hand

THE ART OF SIGN LANGUAGE

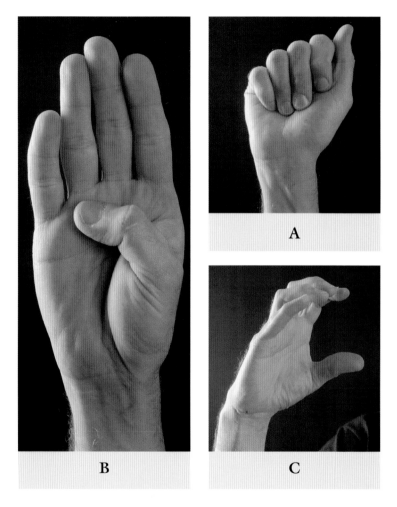

B

A

C

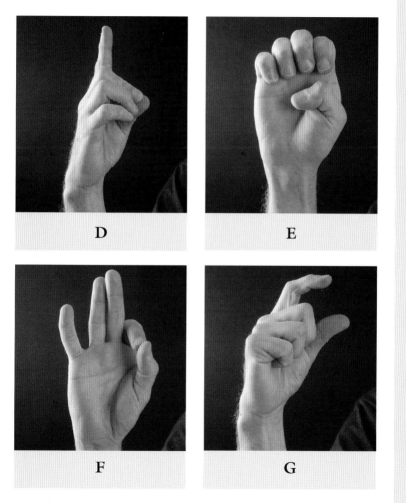

D

E

F

G

manual alphabet & numbers

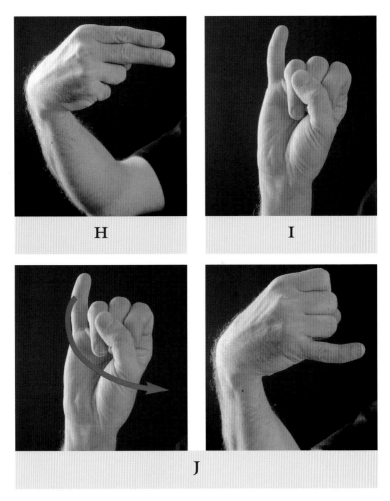

H

I

J

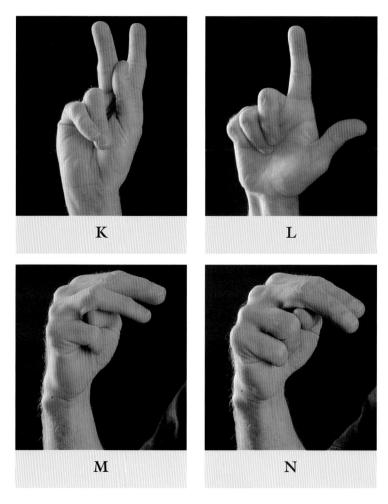

K

L

M

N

13

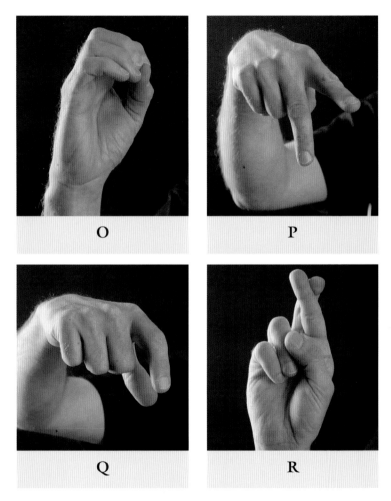

O

P

Q

R

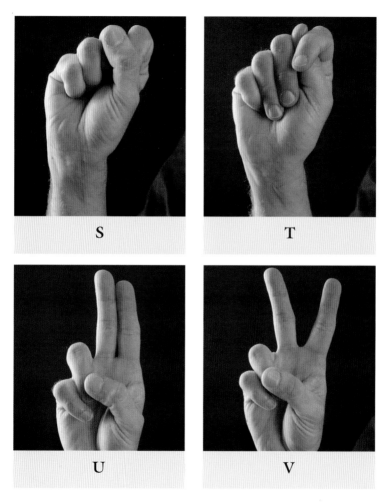

S

T

U

V

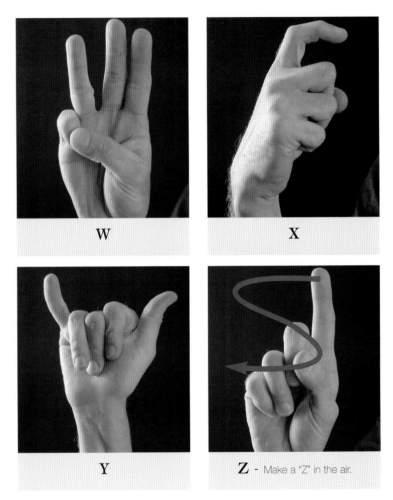

W

X

Y

Z - Make a "Z" in the air.

0

1

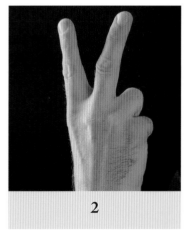

2

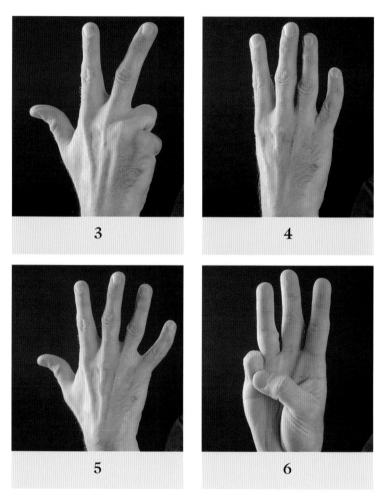

3

4

5

6

THE ART OF SIGN LANGUAGE

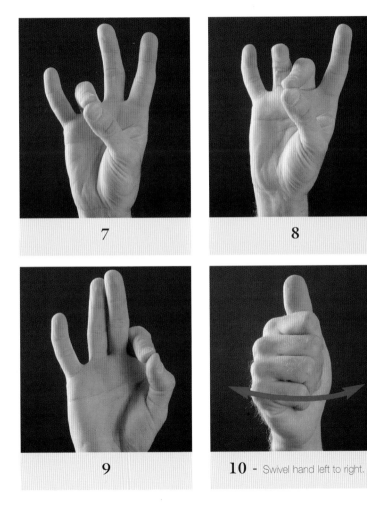

7

8

9

10 - Swivel hand left to right.

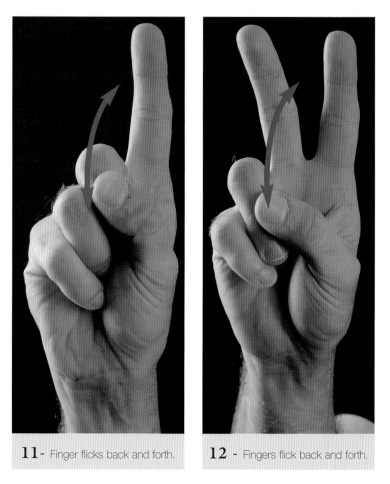

11- Finger flicks back and forth.

12 - Fingers flick back and forth.

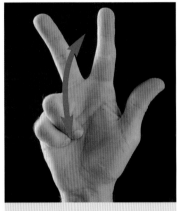

13 - Fingers flick back and forth.

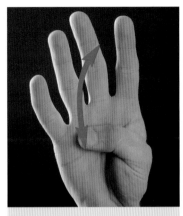

14 - Fingers flick back and forth.

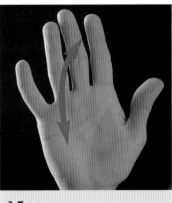

15 - Fingers flick back and forth.

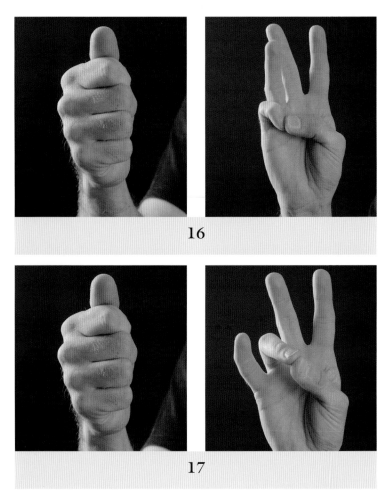

16

17

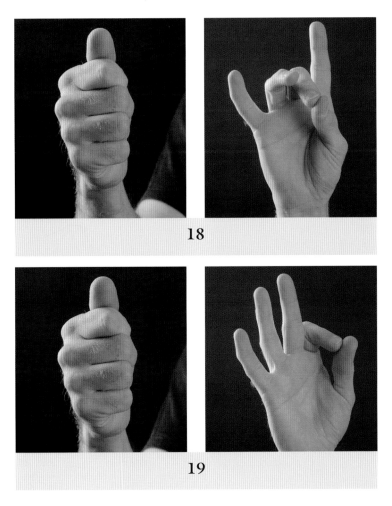

18

19

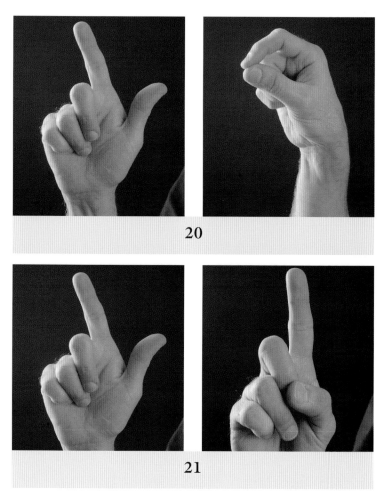

20

21

22 - Move hand to right

23

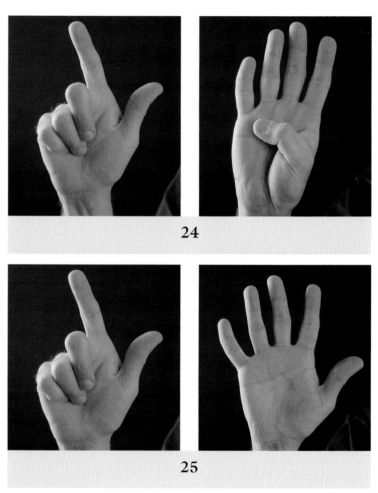

24

25

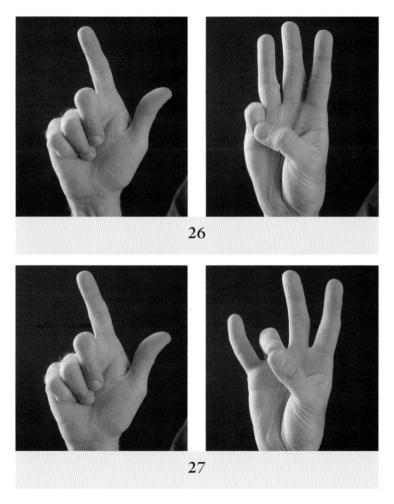

26

27

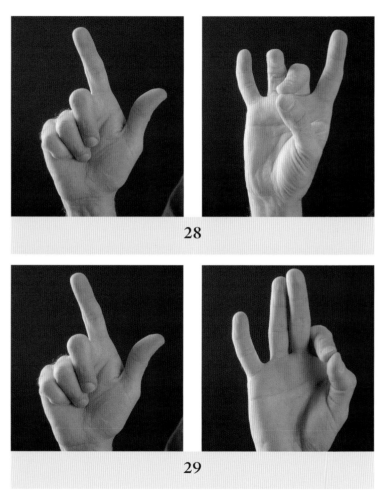

28

29

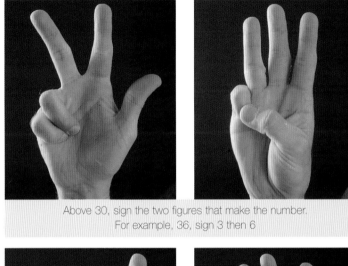

Above 30, sign the two figures that make the number.
For example, 36, sign 3 then 6

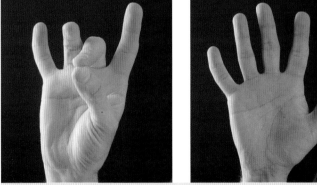

For example, 85, sign 8 then 5

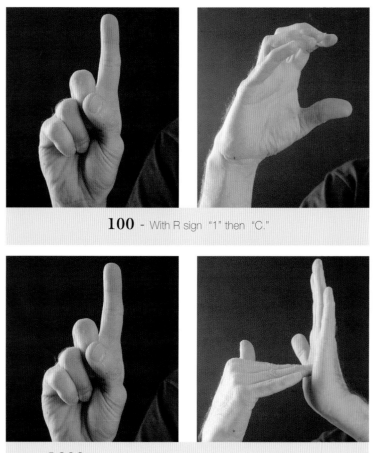

100 - With R sign "1" then "C."

1000 - With R sign "1" then place tips of R "M" in L palm.

1,000,000
With R sign "1" then place tips of
R "M" in L palm and bounce
up palm once.

Please note that although sign markers are used for what may be considered to be regular parts of speech, there are exceptions to all rules. For example, when considering plurals, not all nouns in English take an "–s" or "–es" in their plural form. The plural of "mouse" is not "mouses" but "mice."

The same rule applies in Signed English. Instead of incorrectly signing "mouse" with an "–s" suffix, this plural is created by signing "mouse" and repeating the sign.

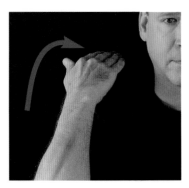

ED (Past)
Wave flat R hand over R shoulder.
E.g. He looked back.

ED (Past alternative)
Sign "D" with R.
Use as alternative to the above.

EN (Past)
Sign "N" with R
E.g. She has taken the book.

THE ART OF SIGN LANGUAGE

32

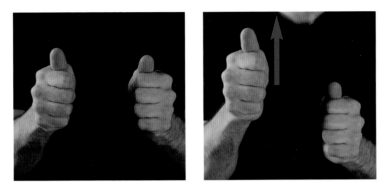

ER (Comparative)
Sign "A" with both hands facing each other, move R up slightly above left
E.g. This house is larger.

EST (Superlative)
Sign "A" with both hands facing each
other, raise R high above the left.
E.g. You are the greatest.

sign markers

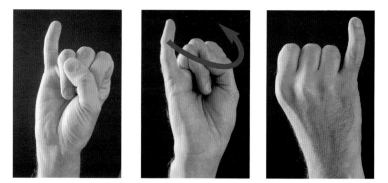

ING (Present Participle)

Sign "I" facing L and twist to R.
E.g. Sitting down.

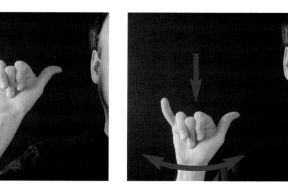

LY (Adverb)

Sign "I Love You" (hand shape) and move down in wavy position.
E.g. He ran quickly.

THE ART OF SIGN LANGUAGE

34

NESS

Place "N" sign near top of flat L hand and move down the hand.
E.g. Happiness.

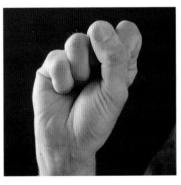

PUNCTUATION

Draw appropriate punctuation mark in
the air with R index finger (or with R
index finger and thumb touching). For
example exclamation mark.

S (Plural)

Sign "S."
E.g. Dogs.

35

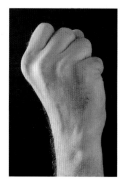

'S OR S'

Face "S" to L and twist to R.
The girl's book or the boys' bicycles.

Y

Sign "Y."
E.g. sleepy.

THE ART OF SIGN LANGUAGE

36

A
Sign "A" move hand to right.

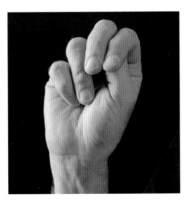 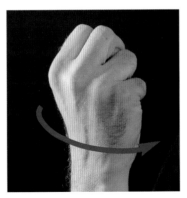

AN
Sign "A", sign "N."

prepositions, questions, articles, & expressions

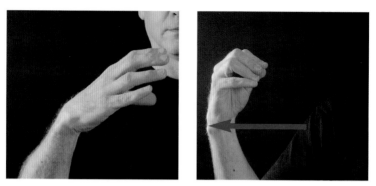

AND

Open R hand, closing slowly as hand drawn to right.

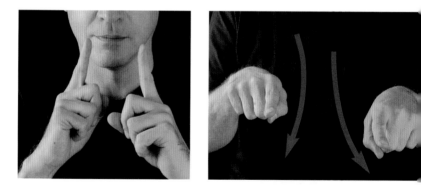

ANSWER

R index finger on mouth, L index finger in front of face,
move both fingers forward in arc.

ANY

R thumb up, swing out to R.

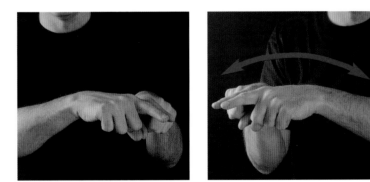

AS

Point both index fingers out close together then move both in arc, left to right.

ASK

Palm together tips out, swing back towards body.

BECAUSE

R fingers on forehead, move to R closing into sign "A."

BUT
Cross index fingers palms out then move apart.

BYE BYE
Wave goodbye.

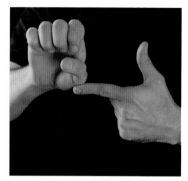

EITHER

Sign "L" with L pointing R, then sign for "E" with R place on L thumb and move to tip of L index finger.

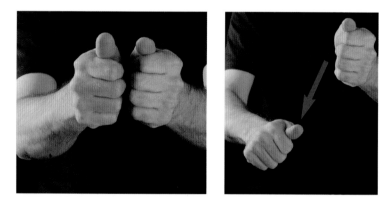

EVERY

Sign "A" with both thumbs up, brush right knuckles of R "A" down knuckles of L.

EXCEPT

Pull L index finger up.

FOR

R index finger on forehead palm in, twist palm out.

43

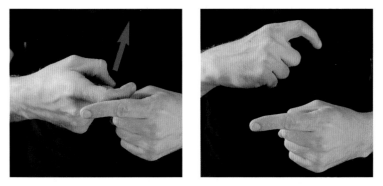

FROM

R "X" sign placed against knuckle of L "X" sign and move R "X" sign back towards body.

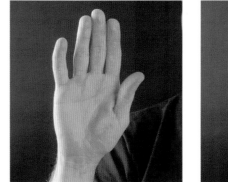

HI

Wave hand.

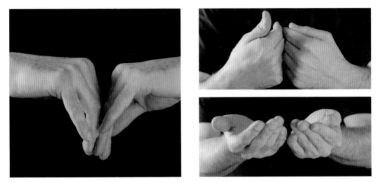

HOW

Hold backs of fingers together with palms down, turn in and up.

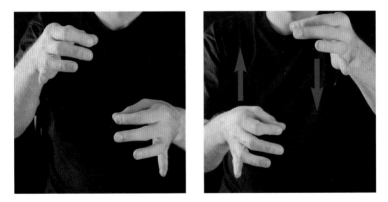

IF

Make "F" sign with both hands facing each other, move up and down.

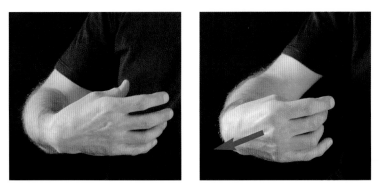

LIKE

Place R index finger and thumb on chest, close together moving away from body.

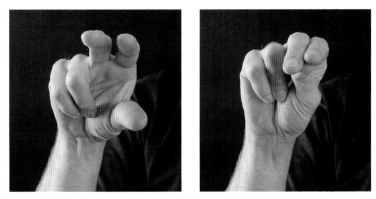

NO

Snap R index finger, middle finger, and thumb quickly together.

THE ART OF SIGN LANGUAGE

46

OK
Fingerspell.

PLEASE
Rub R palm clockwise against chest.

QUESTION
Form question mark in the air with R index finger.

SORRY
Circle "S" sign clockwise on chest.

47

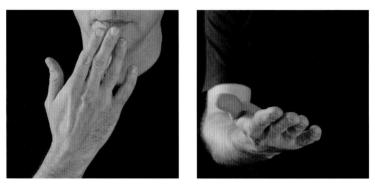

THANK YOU
Touch R hand to lips as though blowing a kiss.

THE
Form "T" sign with R palm out and move from left to right.

WHAT
Brush R index finger across open L fingers.

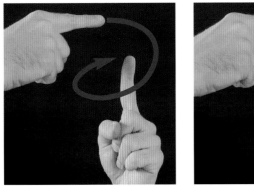

WHEN
Move R index finger around L index finger and then touch together.

WHERE

Wave R index finger from L to R, palm out.

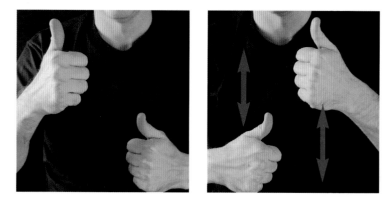

WHICH

Sign "A" with both hands, palms in and thumbs up, alternate up and down.

50

WHO
Move R index finger clockwise around mouth.

WHOSE
Move R index finger clockwise around mouth then sign "S".

WHY
Touch R fingers to forehead palm in and move out into "Y" sign away from body.

51

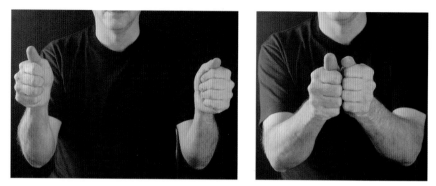

WITH

Sign "A" with both hands thumbs up and knuckles facing, close together.

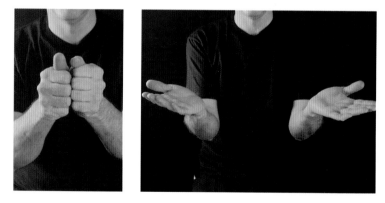

WITHOUT

Sign "A" with both hands knuckles together then draw apart palms up.

THE ART OF SIGN LANGUAGE

52

YES
Sign "S" shake up and down.

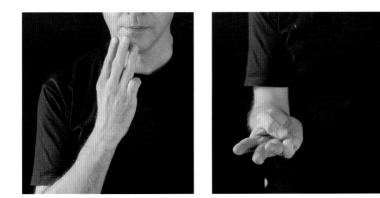

YOU'RE WELCOME
Sign "W" touching fingertips to mouth with palms in and move away from body.

HE
R "E" sign palm L. Place on R temple and move out slightly to the R.

HIS
Place R "S" sign above R eye and move out slightly toward R.

I

Sign "I" with R palm pointing L then moving back against chest.

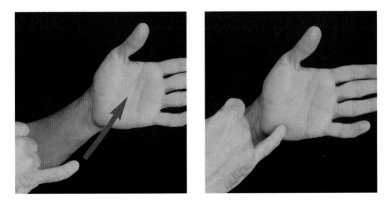

IT

Place tip of R little finger in palm of L hand, L palm facing R.

pronouns

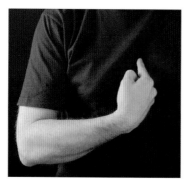

ME
Touch chest with R index finger.

MINE
Slap chest twice with R palm.

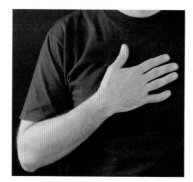

MY
Place R palm on chest.

MYSELF
Make "A" sign with R and twist and tap chest twice.

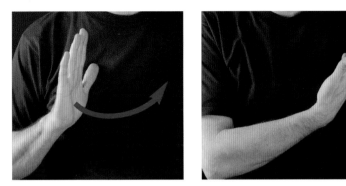

OUR

Arc R hand across chest starting touching R thumb and completing arc with little finger against chest.

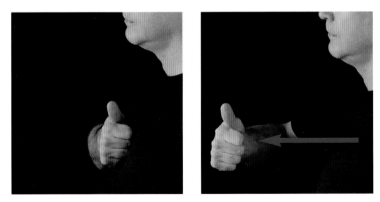

SELF

Sign "A" palm pointing L moving away from body.

SHE

R "E" sign palm L, place on R cheek and move forward.

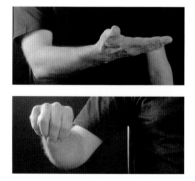 

THEM

Open R hand, palm up, Move from L to R, twisting into an "M" sign.

THEY

Open R hand, palm up. Move from L to R, twisting into a "Y" sign.

THE ART OF SIGN LANGUAGE

58

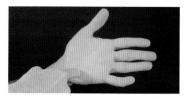

THESE

Open L hand, palm up. Bounce tip of R index finger forward on L palm two or three times.

THOSE

Open L hand, palm up. Tap knuckles of R "Y" sign onto base of L palm and then onto the fingers.

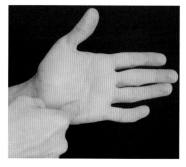

THIS

L hand palm up, fingertips facing away from body, tap L hand with R index finger.

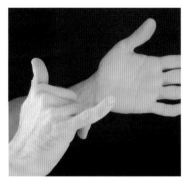 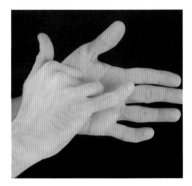

THAT

Place knuckles of R "Y" on L palm.

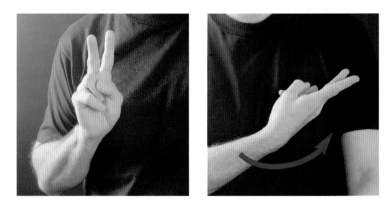

US

Place tips of R "U" sign on R side of chest and arc across to L side of chest.

WE
Touch R index finger on R side of chest and arc across to L side of chest.

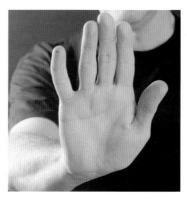

YOU
Point R index finger at person.

YOUR
Push R palm forward to person.

61

AM

Place R "A" sign on mouth and push away from body.

ARE

Place "R" sign on lips and move forward.

CAN

Make "S" sign with both hands, palms down moving downward.

COULD
Make "S" sign with both hands, palms moving downward and repeat movement.

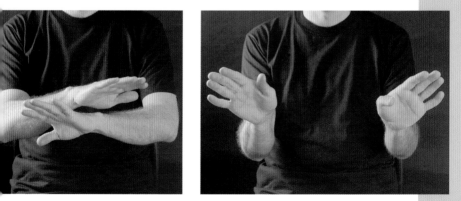

DO NOT/DON'T
Crossed "5" hands, palms facing out and separate and repeat movement.

DOES/DO/DID/DONE

Both hands in front of body, palms down, fingers bent like claws. Hands swing from side to side.

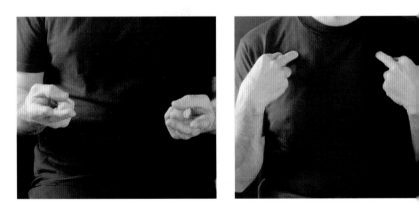

HAVE

"V" sign with both hands, palms in, move towards then touch chest.

IS

R little finger on lips and move away little finger against chest.

SHOULD

"X" sign, palm down, move downward and repeat.

WAS

R "W" sign, move back towards right cheek, close into "S" sign.

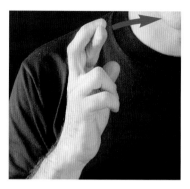

WERE

R "W" sign. Move back towards right cheek, close into "R" sign.

WILL

R palm near R cheek and move forward.

WOULD

Move R "W" sign forward past R side of face and change into a "D" sign.

ABOUT
Point L index finger to R with palm in and circle with R index finger.

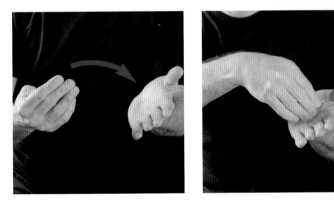

AGAIN
L palm up fingertips out, arc R to left and touch with fingers.

adverbs

67

BACK

L hand open, palm in, fingertips pointing R. Tap back of L hand with R fingertips.

HERE

Both hands, palms up, fingertips pointing up, circle in opposite directions.

LATER

R "L" sign palm L, index finger pointing up, arc forward in a semi-circle.

MAYBE

Both hands palms up, fingertips pointing out, move up and down alternately.

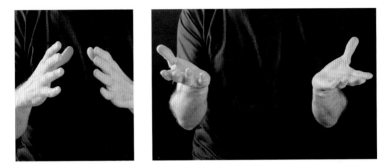

MUCH
Both hands palms facing, close with fingertips together and then separate.

NEVER
R "B" sign palm left and draw downward zigzag in the air.

NOT
"A" sign knuckles L, thumb extended. Place thumb under chin and move forward.

NOW

Both hands, palms up, fingertips bent and lower slightly.

SURE

R "1" sign, place finger on mouth and move away.

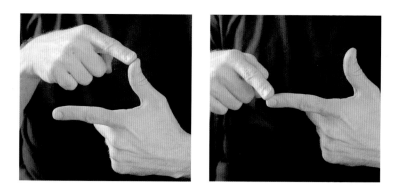

THEN

L "L" sign, thumb up, index finger out. Put R index finger behind thumb and move to tip of index finger.

THERE

Point R index finger out.

TOGETHER

Both hands "A" sign together, palms facing, circle from R to L.

TOO/SAME

"1" sign both hands, palms down, tips facing out, tap together twice.

VERY

L"V" sign both hands, palms facing, touch tips and draw apart.

71

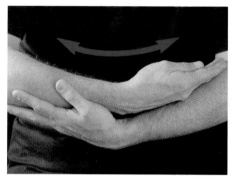

AUNT

R "A" sign palm out, wiggle at side of R cheek.

BABY

Cradle arms at waist level and rock back and forth.

BOY

Snap flat "O" sign twice at forehead with R hand and though touching brim of a hat.

BROTHER

Snap flat "O" sign twice at forehead with R hand, then tap index fingers together, palms down and tips out.

CHILD

Lower R hand, palm down, as if indicating a small child.

CHILDREN

Lower R hand, palm down, as if indicating a small child then bounce to the R.

73

DENTIST

Tap R side of mouth with R "D" sign.

DOCTOR

Flat L hand palm up, tips out, tap L wrist with fingertips of R "M" sign.

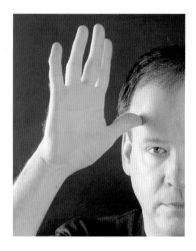

FATHER

R "5" sign, palm left, tap forehead with thumb twice.

THE ART OF SIGN LANGUAGE

74

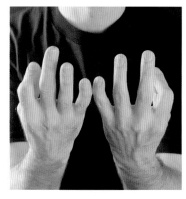

FAMILY

"F" sign both hands, palms out and index fingers touching, draw around and apart until little fingers touch.

FRIEND

Hook R "X" sign over upturned "X" sign and reverse.

GIRL

R "A" palm L, thumb on cheek and draw down jaw line.

HUSBAND

Place thumb of R "B" palm down at forehead, move down and clasp extended L hand with palm up.

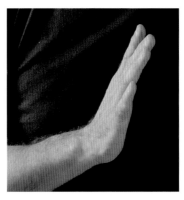

MAN

R "B" sign palm L, touch thumb to forehead then arc down to chest.

MOTHER

R "5" sign, palm L, fingertips up, tap chin with thumb twice.

NEPHEW

R "U" sign, wiggle at R temple.

77

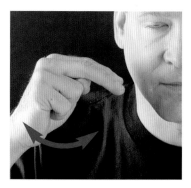

NIECE

Shake R "N" sign at R jaw line.

NURSE

Flat L hand palm up, tips out, tap L wrist with fingertips of R "N" sign twice.

PARENT

R "P" sign, place middle finger on R side of forehead and then on chin.

PEOPLE

Both hands "P" sign palms out, move down alternately up and down in circular motion.

PERSON

Both hands "P" sign palms down, fingertips out, wrists against side of body and move out.

POLICE

Tap R "C" sign below L shoulder.

79

SISTER

R thumb on R cheek, then tap both index fingers together, palms down and tips out.

UNCLE

R "U" sign wiggle at R temple.

WIFE

Descend R thumb down R cheek, then clasp hands together.

WOMAN

Descend R thumb down R side of chin, then open hand and place thumb against chest.

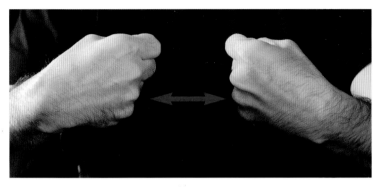

ACCIDENT
"S" sign both hands knuckles facing, strike together.

ARM
Grab L wrist with R "C" sign and move along arm to elbow.

BAND AID
L "S" sign, draw R "H" sign over back of "S" sign.

82

BEARD

Grasp chin with R hand and move down to "O" sign.

BELT

Move index fingers and thumbs from each side of waist to middle of stomach, as if fastening a buckle.

BLIND

Touch eyes with R "V" sign.

BLOOD

L hand palm in, tips R. Trickle R fingers down back of L hand to indicate dripping blood.

about the body (nouns)

83

BLOUSE

Both hands palm down at upper chest. Arc down to lower chest, palms up, little fingers touching against chest.

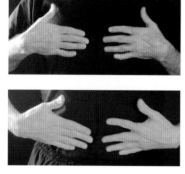

BODY

Both hands palms in, tips facing. Pat upper chest then stomach.

BOOT

L hand palm down, tips out. Place in R "C" sign, then slide "C" sign up to elbow.

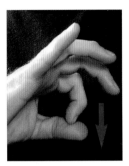

BUTTON

Curve R index finger inside thumb, tap chest three times moving downward.

CLOTHES

Both hands palms in, brush down chest twice.

COLD

Grasp nose with thumb and index finger of R hand, then move away as if using a handkerchief.

COAT

"A" sign both hands, palms in. Trace shape of lapels with thumbs.

85

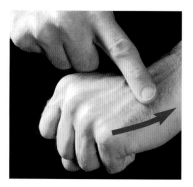

CUT

L "S" sign palm down, draw R index finger across back of L.

DEAF

Point R index finger to ear, place index fingers of both hands together with palms down.

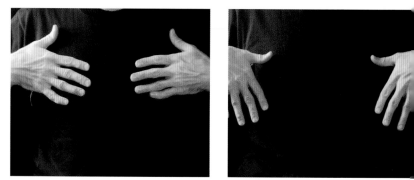

DRESS

Both hands palms in, brush tips down chest spreading fingers apart slightly.

EAR

Pinch R ear lobe with thumb and index finger.

EMERGENCY

R "E" sign palm out, shake from side to side.

FACE

Circle face with index finger.

87

FEVER

R hand palm out tips L, place back of hand on forehead.

FOOT

L hand palm down tips R. R "F" sign thumb and index finger on L thumb and circle around to L little finger.

GLASSES

Thumb and index fingers of both hands on side of eyes. Move away closing fingers as if outlining glasses frame.

88

GLOVE
Place R hand over L palm, tips out fingers interlocking. Then draw R hand back along L palm.

HAIR
Grab strand of hair with R thumb and index finger.

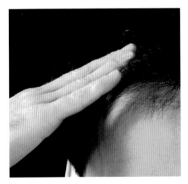

HAT
Pat top of head.

HEAD
R hand palm down tips L. Place tips on R temple then move down to chin.

HEARING AID

R thumb, index finger and middle finger placed on the ear as if inserting a hearing aid.

HEART

Tap heart with R middle finger.

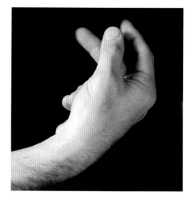

INJECTION

Back of R "V" sign, thumb extended. Then mime giving injection.

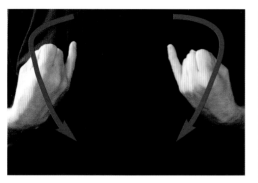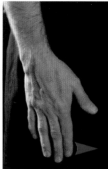

JACKET

"I" sign both hands, palms in. Touch index fingers to chest and move down outlining lapels.

LEG

Pat R thigh with R hand.

MEDICINE

Circle R middle finger on L upturned palm.

MENTALLY RETARDED

Tap R side of head with "M" sign and "R" sign.

91

MIND
Tap R temple with "M" sign.

MOUTH
Outline mouth with R index finger.

NECK
Tap neck with R hand palm down.

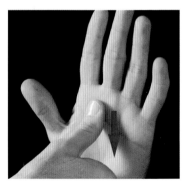

OPERATION
L hand palm out, tips up. Draw tip of R thumb down L palm.

PANTS

Place palms of both hands on hips and brush up towards waist.

PILL

Mime taking a pill with thumb and index finger.

PREGNANT

Interlock fingers of both hands and move away from stomach.

PURSE

Mime holding purse.

93

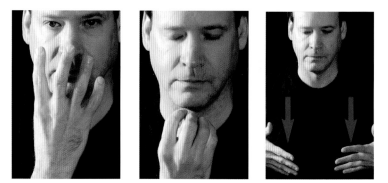

PAJAMAS

Draw R fingers down face ending in "O" sign. Both hands palms in, tips facing, place on upper chest and move down.

RING

Place R index finger and thumb around L ring finger and mime putting on a ring.

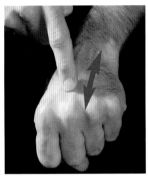

ROBE

"R" sign both hands, palms in, tips facing. Brush down chest.

SCRATCH

Scratch back of L hand with R index finger.

SHIRT

Tug shirt between thumb and forefinger.

SHOE

"S" sign both hands palms down. Strike together several times.

SHORTS

Both hands palms up, fingertips on inside of thighs and move outward, outlining bottom of shorts.

SICK

Tap forehead with R middle finger.

SKIRT

Both hands palms down, thumbs on waist, brush down.

SLIPPER

L "C" sign, palm down. R hand palm down, tips left. Slide R through L "C" sign.

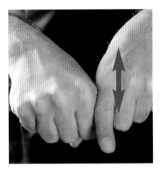

SOCK

"S" sign R hand palm down. Brush back and forth along side of L index finger, palm down.

SORE

"S" sign both hands palm down, twist in opposite direction while moving towards each other.

STOMACH

Pat stomach with R hand.

SUNGLASSES

Circle R and L index fingers around eyes.

97

TEETH
Outline teeth with bent index finger.

TEMPERATURE
"1" sign both hands, L palm out, R palm down. Rub R index finger up and down L.

THERMOMETER
L "L" sign palm out. R "T" sign knuckles L. Rub "T" up and down L index finger.

TROUBLE
Both hands, palms facing slanted outward. Circle inward in front of the face.

UMBRELLA

"S" sign both hands, palms in, R on L. R hand moves up.

VOICE

R "V" sign palm in. Place tips on throat and arc outward.

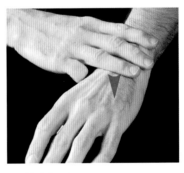

VOMIT

"5" sign both hands, palms facing, R thumb on mouth. Move hands downward sharply.

WATCH

L hand palm down, tips L. Tap wrist with R "M" sign.

BRUSH HAIR

Brush knuckles of R "A" sign down hair twice.

BRUSH TEETH

Rub R index finger back and forth across teeth.

CARRY

Both hands open, palms up, tips slanted left. Move from L to R or R to L.

CATCH

Go through the motion of catching a ball.

CLOSE

"B" sign both palms facing, tips out, arc index fingers together.

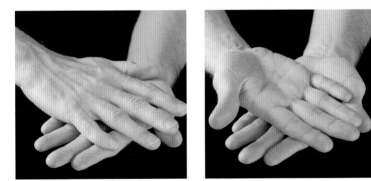

COOK

L hand palm up, R hand palm down. Put R palm on L and flip over as if flipping pancakes.

about the body (verbs)

CRY

Place index fingers under eyes, slide fingers down cheeks showing where tears would flow.

DANCE

L hand palm up, tips out. Sweep R "V" sign over palm several times.

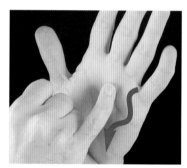

DRAW

L palm tips up facing R, make a wavy drawing motion with R little finger down L palm.

DRINK

Bring R "C" sign to mouth as if holding a glass.

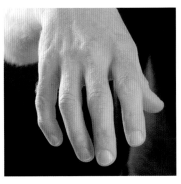

DROP

Hold R "S" sign at shoulder level palm down and open fingers as if dropping something.

EAT

Place tips of R hand on lips and replace several times.

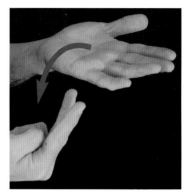

FALL

L hand palm up tips out. Place tips of R "V" sign on L palm then flip forward and out ending with palm up.

FIGHT

"S" sign both hands knuckles facing, cross in front of body several times.

THE ART OF SIGN LANGUAGE

104

HEAR
Point R index
finger to ear.

HIT
Left "1" sign palm R, strike L
index finger with R fist.

HOLD
"S" sign both hands
palms in. Place R on
top of L as if grasp-
ing something.

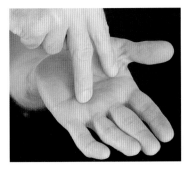
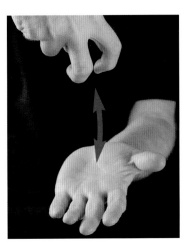

JUMP
L palm up tips out, place tips of R "V"
sign in L palm and pull up changing
into a bent "V" and repeat.

105

LAUGH

Place index fingers of both hands on sides of the mouth and flick out two or three times.

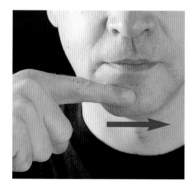

LIE

Push R index finger across chin from R to L.

LISTEN

Cup R hand over R ear.

LOOK

Point at eyes with R "V" sign, twist and point forward.

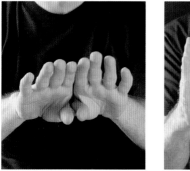 

OPEN

"B" sign both hands palms down tips out and touching index fingers. Pull apart ending palms up, palms facing each other.

POUR
"A" sign R hand, arc left L pointing thumb towards ground.

PULL
"A" sign both hands knuckles up. Place L hand ahead of R and pull towards body quickly.

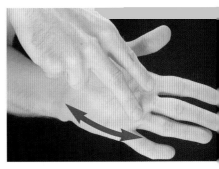

PUSH
Both hands tips up, palms out, L in front of R. Push out.

READ
L hand tips up palm facing R, move tips of R "V" sign down left palm and move back and forth.

RUN

"L" sign both hands index finger pointing out, L forward of R. Hook R index finger around L thumb, wiggle fingers while pushing both hands forward.

SAY

"I" sign R hand palm in, tip pointing L. Hold at mouth and circle forward.

SEE

"V" sign R hand palm in, place tips at eyes then move forward.

SIGN (Language)

"I" sign both hands palms out. Alternate circular motions towards body.

SING

L hand palm up tips right, swing fingers of R hand back and forth over palm.

SIT

"H" sign both hands palms down, L hand pointing slightly R, R hand pointing slightly L. Rest R fingers on L fingers.

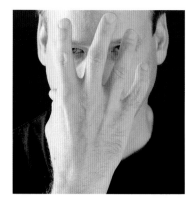

SLEEP

Draw R "5" sign palm in. Slide down face ended with fingers together.

SMILE
Place index fingers of both hands on sides of mouth and move up to cheeks.

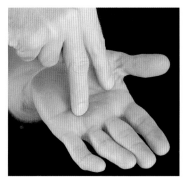

STAND
L hand palm up, tips out. Stand tips of R "V" sign on L palm.

TALK
Place index fingers on mouth alternately moving back and forth.

111

TASTE

"5" shape R hand palm in, tap middle finger on chin.

TEACH

Hold both hands at temples as if grasping mortarboard, hold at temples and move out twice.

WAKE UP

Hold index finger and thumbs of both hands over eyes, knuckles facing each other, open into "L" signs.

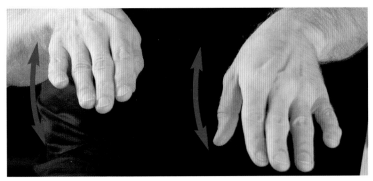

WALK

Both hands palms down tips out. Flap alternately as if doing a doggy paddle.

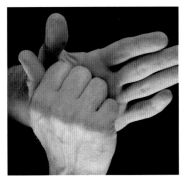

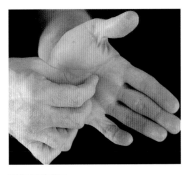

WRITE

L hand palm out tips up, mime writing on L palm with closed R index finger and thumb.

WASH

L hand palm up tips out, rub R "S" sign on upturned L palm.

113

ATTENTION

Both hands palms in placed on temples, move forward in parallel to each other.

BASKET

Place R index finger under L wrist and swing to elbow. End with little finger touching.

BATH

Both hands knuckle in thumbs up, scrub chest.

BED

Tilt head slightly with R palm on R cheek.

BELL

L hand tips up and palm R, strike with R "S" sign knuckles down. Repeat.

BLACK

Draw R index finger across forehead from L to R.

BLANKET

Both hands palms down, fingertips facing. Move up chest.

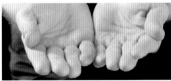

BLUE

R "B" sign palm L, shake back and forth.

BOOK

Palms together thumbs up, open as if opening a book.

school & home

115

BOX

Both hands palms facing thumbs up, form a box by turning L hand R and R hand L.

BROWN

R hand, palm L, tips up. Place on R cheek and slide down.

CAMERA

Mime taking a photograph.

THE ART OF SIGN LANGUAGE

116

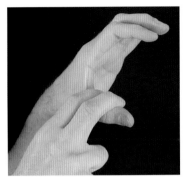

CANDLE

R hand palm forward tips up. Place tip of L index finger on R wrist and wiggle fingers of R hand.

CHAIR

L "C" sign palm facing R, hook R "N" sign palm forward over L thumb.

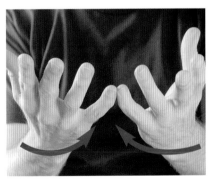

CLASS

Both hands "C" shape held close together with palms out. Draw around in an arc to the front and forward, complete arc with little fingers touching and palms in.

117

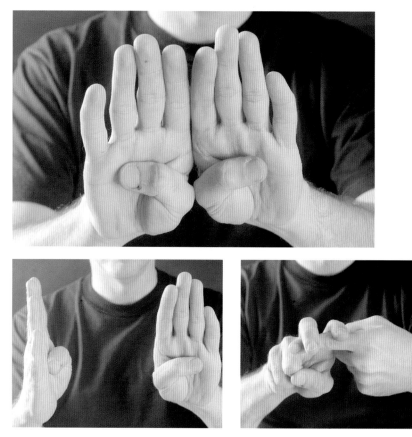

CLOSET

"B" sign both hands, index fingers touching. Turn R hand R, palm will face L then hook R index finger over base of L index finger and move forward.

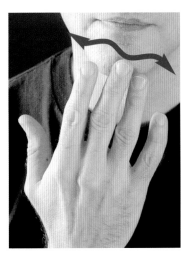

COLOR

R "5" sign, palm in, wiggle fingers at chin level.

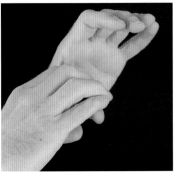

COUCH

Both hands "C" sign, L palm out, R palm to L. Hook R "C" over thumb of L "C."

CRAYON

L hand palm up, tips out. R "C" sign, move R thumb forward on L palm with wavy motion.

119

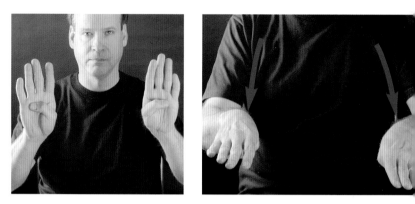

CURTAIN

Both hands "4" sign, drop forward and down ending with palms down.

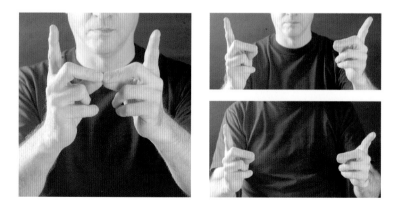

DESK

"D" sign both hands palms facing, draw apart and down.

THE ART OF SIGN LANGUAGE

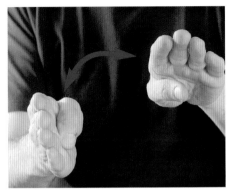

DOOR

"B" sign both hands palms out, tips slightly raised with index finger together. Then turn R to R ending with palm L and return to starting position.

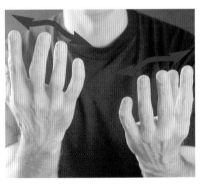

DRAWER

With cupped hands mime opening a drawer.

FIRE

Both hands "R" sign palms in, move up wiggling fingers.

121

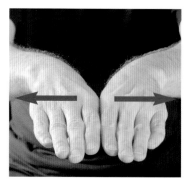

FLOOR

Both hands "B" sign, palms out, index fingers touching. Move apart.

GREEN

R "G" sign, shake back and forth.

HAMMER

L "S" sign knuckles R, R "A" sign moves towards L as if hitting a nail.

KITCHEN

R "K" sign, shake back and forth.

THE ART OF SIGN LANGUAGE

122

LAMP

R hand palm down tips L, place R elbow in L upturned palm. Open R fingers into a "5" sign, palm down.

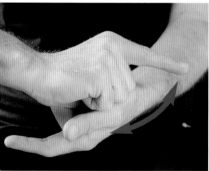

LAUNDRY

"L" sign both hands, L hand palm up tips R, R hand palm down tips L. Twist back and forth.

123

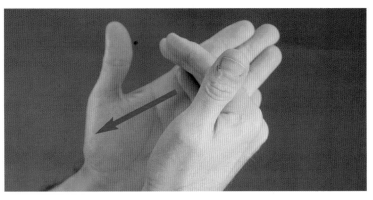

LESSON

L hand palm up tips out with R hand fingers bent. Place R on fingertips and heel of L hand.

LETTER

Place thumb of R "A" sign on mouth then on upturned L palm.

THE ART OF SIGN LANGUAGE

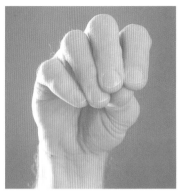
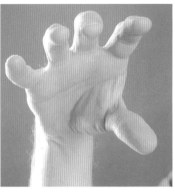

LIGHT

R hand fingertips together palm down. Open fingers into "5" sign, palm down.

MAIL

Thumb of R "A" sign on mouth, change to R "M" sign, and place fingertips on upturned L palm.

125

MEETING

"5" sign both hands, palms facing, tips up. Bring together, tips touching.

MIRROR

With R hand, palm in front of face, twist slightly to R and repeat.

MUSIC

L hand palm up, tips slightly R. Swing R "M" sign back and forth over L palm and forearm without touching.

THE ART OF SIGN LANGUAGE

126

NOISE

"5" sign both hands held at ears, palms out. Shake outward.

ORANGE

R "C" sign palms and tips L. Place at mouth and squeeze into an "S" shape and repeat.

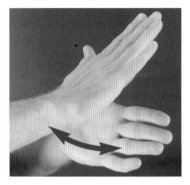

OVEN

L hand palm down tips R. Slide R hand palm up under L.

PAPER

L hand palm up tips out, R hand palm down tips L. Brush R palm across L palm twice towards the body.

PENCIL

L hand palm up tips R. Touch tips of R thumb and index finger to mouth, then slide across L palm.

THE ART OF SIGN LANGUAGE

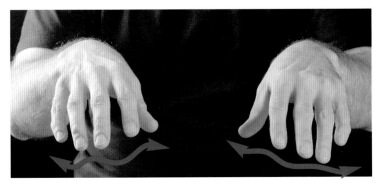

PIANO
Mime playing piano keyboard.

PICTURE
L hand open palm R, tips up. Place R "C" sign against R eye, then move down to L palm.

PILLOW

Place back of L hand at R side of head, tilt head to R, and mime patting underside of pillow with R hand.

PURPLE

R "P" sign, shake back and forth from wrist.

RADIO

Place cupped R hand over R ear.

THE ART OF SIGN LANGUAGE

130

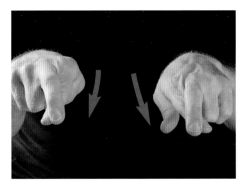

RED

Brush lower lip with tip of
R index finger and repeat.

REFRIDGERATOR

"R"sign both hands tips out, shake back and forth
in shivering motion.

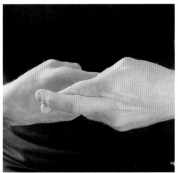

ROOM

"R" shape both hands tips out, palms facing. Turn R hand to L and L hand to R
to form box shape, hands finish opposite each other.

131

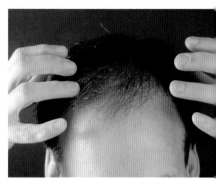

SCISSORS

"V" sign R hand, palms in tips left. Mime cutting with scissors.

SHAMPOO

Place tips of both hands on head and rub back and forth as if shampooing hair.

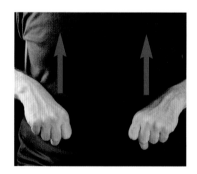

SHEET

Both hands "S" sign knuckles down. Move up from waist to shoulders as if pulling up a sheet.

SHELF

Both hands palms down, tips out, held high at shoulder level. Hold together and move apart in straight line.

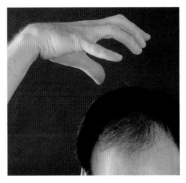

SHOWER

R "S" sign held above the head and open into a "5" sign and repeat.

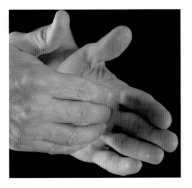

SOAP

L hand palm up tips out, R palm in tips down. Draw R fingers backwards across L palm ending in "A" sign.

133

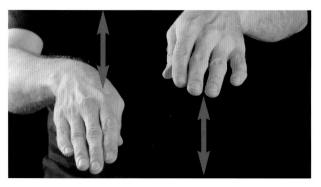

STAIRS
Both hands tips out palms down, alternate upward steps.

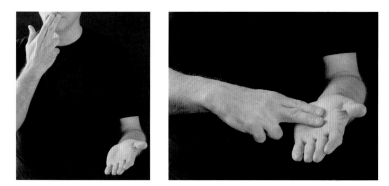

STAMP
L hand palm up tips out. Place tips of R "H" sign on lips and then move down to L palm.

134

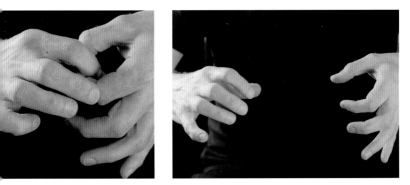

STORY

Join "F" sign of both hands like links in a chair and then separate a few times.

STRING

"S" sign L hand palm out. Place tip of R "I" sign on L "S" and shake away to R.

135

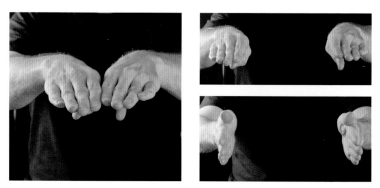

TABLE

Both hands palms down tips out, index fingers touching. Draw apart and down miming shape of a table.

TAPE

"H" sign both hands palms down tips touching. Move apart in a straight line.

TELEPHONE

R "Y" sign, place thumb on ear and little finger on mouth.

TELEVISION

Fingerspell "T.V."

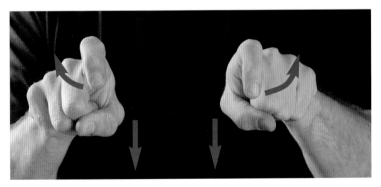

TEST

"X" sign both hands palms out. Hook and unhook both index fingers several times moving hands downward.

THING

R hand palm up, tips out. Move out and to R in small bouncing movements.

TOILET

Shake R "T" sign several times from L to R.

TOOTHBRUSH

Rub edge of mouth with R index finger.

TOOTHPASTE

Mime spreading paste on toothbrush.

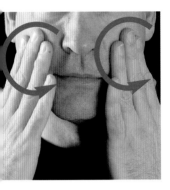

TOWEL

Both hands palms in tips up. Circle fingertips on cheeks.

VACATION

"5" sign both hands facing, tips out. Tap upper chest with thumbs several times.

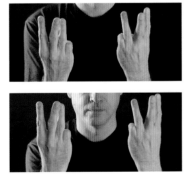

WALL

"W" sign both hands, palms in and held close together. Move apart and back outlining the shape of a wall.

139

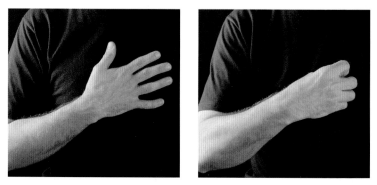

WHITE
R "5" sign palms in, tips L. Place R tips on chest and draw out into "O" sign.

WINDOW
Both hands palms in, tips opposite. Place R on top of L little fingers touching. Move R hand up and down.

YELLOW
R "Y" sign, shake in and out.

THE ART OF SIGN LANGUAGE

140

BALL
Place tips of hands together outlining the shape of a ball.

BALLOON
"S" sign both hands, place at mouth, L in front of R. Move apart as if forming a large balloon.

BASEBALL
Mime grasping a bat and swinging it at a ball.

leisure

141

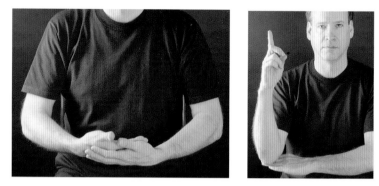

BIRTHDAY

R "4" sign, palms in tips L. Place on upper L arm then flip over L forearm.

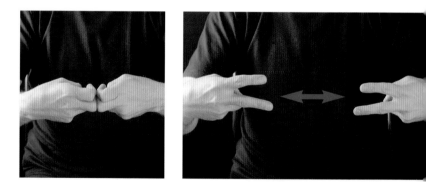

BOW

"V" sign both hands palms in, place knuckles together and draw apart into straight "V" signs.

THE ART OF SIGN LANGUAGE

142

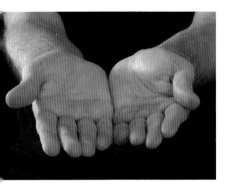

CARD
Palms up and hands together like an opened book.

CHRISTMAS
Place elbow of R "C" sign on back of L hand which is held in front pointing tips R. Arc R "C" from R to L.

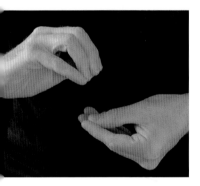

DECORATE
Flat "O" sign both hands, L palm up, R palm down. Touch tips and reverse positions several times.

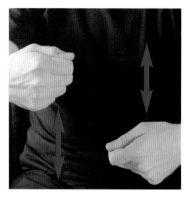

DRUM

Mime holding drumsticks and beating a drum.

EASTER

"E" shape both hands, circle away from each other.

FOOTBALL

"5" sign both hands palms in tips facing. Link fingers together several times.

GAME

"A" shape both hands palm in, thumbs up. Hit knuckles together once while moving hands downward.

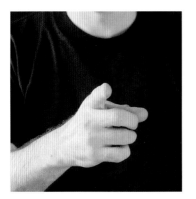

GOD

Point R "G" sign upward, move back down to chest ending in "B" sign.

HORN

L "C" sign, palms and tips R. R "S" sign palm left. Hold R at mouth and blow.

JESUS

"B" sign open both hands, palms in tips out. Place tip of R middle finger of L palm, then place tip of L middle finger on R palm.

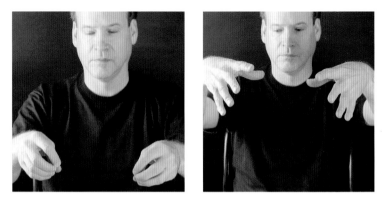

MAGIC

Flat "O" sign both hands tips out, move away from the body in a semi-circle opening into a "5" sign, palms out tips down.

MERRY

Both hands palms in, tips facing. Brush up the chest twice.

PARTY

"P" sign both hands palms down, swing hand simultaneously to L and R several times.

PRAY

Place palms together tips up, rotate towards body.

PRESENT

"P" shape both hands, bring up and turn out.

PUZZLE

"A" sign both hands thumbs down, place them together as if trying to achieve a fit.

REINDEER

"R" sign both hands thumbs extended, palms out. Place thumbs on temples move up and out.

ROPE

"R" sign both hands, palms in tips touching. Draw apart.

SANTA CLAUS

"C" sign R hand palm in. With index finger in, arc down to chest.

SLEIGH

"X" sign both hands, palms in. Arc outward ending with palm up and draw back towards the body.

SLIDE

R hand palm down held at shoulder. Bring down in swooping motion.

SURPRISE

Place both index fingers and thumbs at edges of eyes. Snap open into "L" signs.

149

SWING

Hook R "V" sign over L "H" sign, palms down. Mime swinging back and forth.

TENNIS

Mime swinging a tennis racket.

THANKSGIVING

Both hands open palms in. Place tips on the mouth, then arc out and down then up again.

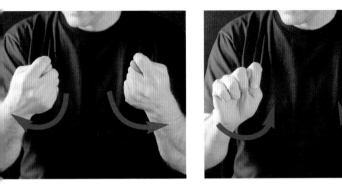

TOY
"T" sign both hands, swing in and out twice.

VALENTINE
Make shape of a heart on L chest with tips of "V" sign with both hands.

WRAP
Both hands palms in, L tips R, R tips L. Circle L hand around R.

ACT

"A" sign both hands, palms facing. Move back in circles brushing thumbs down chest.

BREAK

"S" signs both hands, palms down, thumbs and index fingers touching. Then separate.

152

BRING

Both hands palms up, one slightly behind the other. Mime carrying an item towards the body.

BURN

L "1" sign, palm down, tip R. Wiggle fingers of R hand beneath L finger.

BUY

Place back of R palm in L palm and move forward.

actions

153

CHANGE

"A" sign both hands, L palm up, R palm down. Place R wrist on L wrist and then reverse.

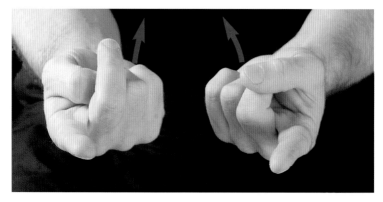

COME

"1" sign both hands, palms up tips out. Bring tips up and back towards chest.

CUT

R "V" sign, palms in tips L. Mime cutting with scissors.

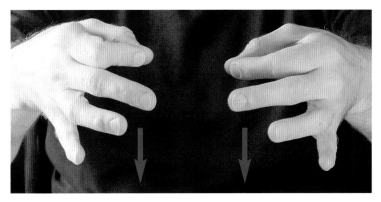

DECIDE

"F" sign both hands palms facing. Lower hands.

155

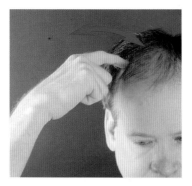

DREAM

Place R index finger on forehead, move away from head crooking finger several times.

FEEL

Tap R middle finger upward on chest.

FIND

R "5" sign, palm down, tips out. Close thumb and index finger and raise hand as if grasping.

FINISH
"5" sign both hands palm in, turn so that palms and tips face out.

FOLLOW
"A" sign both hands, thumbs up, R behind L, move forward together.

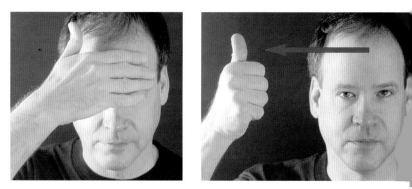

FORGET

R hand palm in, tips L. Draw across forehead from L to R ending in an "A" sign.

GET

"C" sign both hands, right slightly above L. Move towards body closing into "S" signs.

THE ART OF SIGN LANGUAGE

158

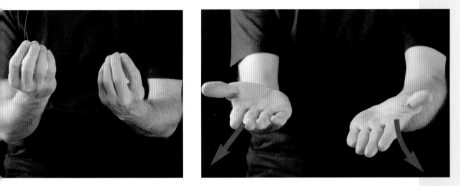

GIVE

"O" sign both hands, palms up, L ahead of R. Move forward opening fingers.

GO

"1" sign both hands, palms and fingertips in. Rotate hands out ending with palms up.

159

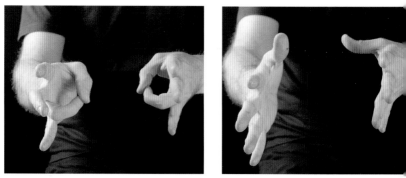

HATE

"8" sign both hands, palms facing each other. Flick middle fingers from thumbs.

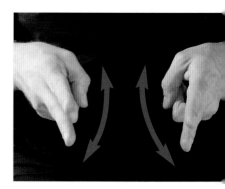

HELP

L "A" sign, palm L, place in R palm and raise R palm up.

HURRY

"H" sign both hands, palms facing, tips out. Shake up and down.

THE ART OF SIGN LANGUAGE

KEEP

"V" sign both hands, tips out. Place R "V" on L "V."

KNOW

R hand palm in, tips up. Tap forehead.

LEARN

L "5" sign, palm up tips out. Place fingertips of R "5" sign in L palm then move to the forehead changing into an "O" sign.

161

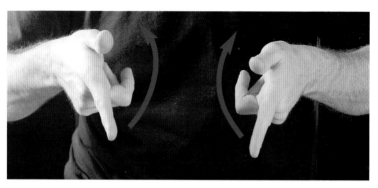

LET

"L" sign both hands, palms facing, tips out and pointing slightly down. Raise to an upright position.

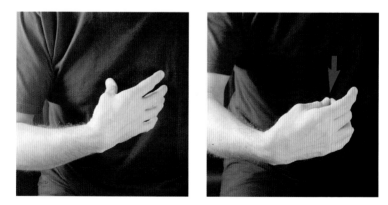

LIKE

Place R middle finger and thumb on chest, move away and close fingers.

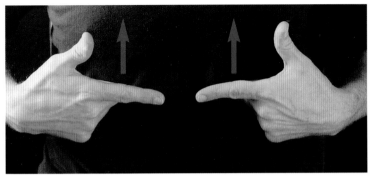

LIVE

"L" sign both hands, palms in, thumbs up. Place on chest and move up.

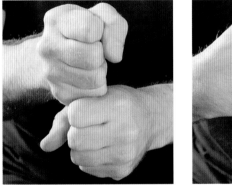

MAKE

"S" sign both hands, palms in. Place R hand on L and twist hands towards body.

163

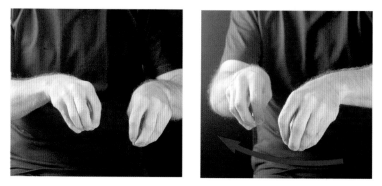

MOVE

"O" sign both hands, palms down. Mime moving something from R to L or L to R.

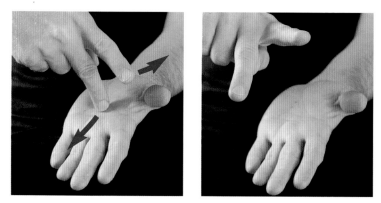

PAY

L hand palm up, tips out. Place middle finger of R hand on L palm and flick out.

PLAY
"Y" sign both hands palms in, twist both back and forth.

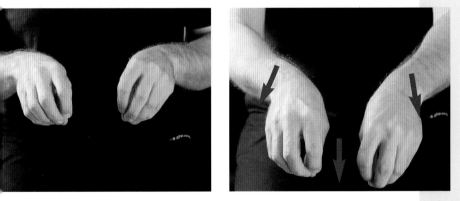

PUT
"O" sign both hands palms down, move forward and down.

REMEMBER

Place thumb of R "A" sign on forehead, then drop down and touch thumb of L "A" sign.

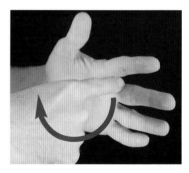

SHOP

L hand palm up, tips out. Place back of R "O" sign on L palm and move out twice.

START

L "5" sign palm R. Place R index finger between L and middle finger and make half turn.

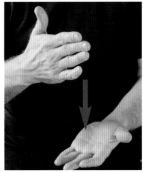

STAY

"A" sign both hands, palms in. Place R thumb on L thumb and push down together.

STOP

L hand palm up, tips out. Strike R hand with palm L down onto L palm.

TAKE

R "5" sign palm down. Draw up quickly ending in an "S" sign.

167

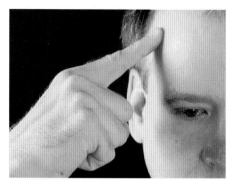

THINK
Place tip of R index finger on forehead.

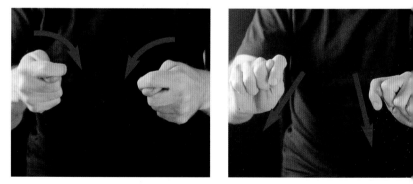

TRY
"T" sign both hands palms facing. Move forward and arc downward.

168

THE ART OF SIGN LANGUAGE

UNDERSTAND
R "S" sign palm in. Place near R temple and snap index finger up.

VISIT
"V" sign both hands palm in, circle away from the body.

WAIT
Both hands palms up, tips out in front of the body and L slightly forward. Wiggle fingers.

169

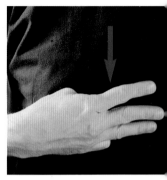

WANT

"5" sign both hands, palms up, fingers curved. Move back towards body.

WISH

"W" sign R hand, palms in. Place on chest and move down.

WORK

"S" sign both hands, palms down. Hit back of L "S" sign with R "S" sign and repeat.

WORRY

"W" sign both hands, palms slanted out. Circle alternately in front of face.

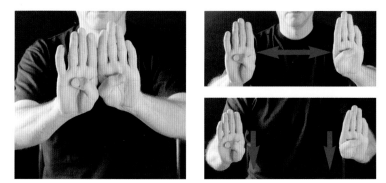

BARN

"B" sign both hands palms out and touching. Draw the shape of a barn, apart and down.

BEACH

"B" sign both hands palms down, L tips slanted R, R tips slanted L. Circle R hand over L up to elbow and back.

BEAR
Cross wrists of clawed hands and scratch upper chest.

BIRD
"G" sign R hand, tips L. Place on chin and snap index finger and thumb together twice.

BUTTERFLY
Hook both thumbs together palms in and flap fingers.

CAT
Place R "9" sign on side of mouth and pull away twice.

THE ART OF SIGN LANGUAGE

172

CHICKEN

Place side of R "G" sign on mouth, then place tips in L palm.

COW

Place thumb of R "Y" sign on R temple then twist forward.

DIRT

Place back of R hand with tips L under chin and wiggle fingers.

173

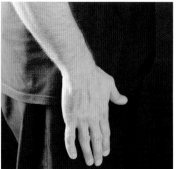

DOG

Slap R thigh with R hand twice, then snap R thumb and middle finger twice.

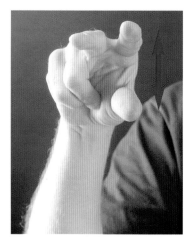

DUCK

Snap thumb, middle finger, and index finger at the mouth to indicate a quacking duck.

FARM

"5" sign R hand, palm in, tips L. Place thumb on L side of chin and draw across to R side.

FENCE

"4" sign both hands, palm in, tips facing. Place tips of middle fingers together then draw apart.

FISH

"B" sign both hands, L palm R, R palm L. Place tips of L hand on R wrist. Flutter R while moving forward.

FLOWER

R "O" sign, place tips on R side of nose then arc to L side of nose.

175

GARDEN

"G" sign both hands tips out, then move R in front of L to indicate a square.

GOOSE

L "B" sign palms down tips R, R "G" sign, rest R elbow on back of L hand.

NATURE   GRASS – GROWegment>

GRASS

L "B" sign palms out, tips R. R "G" sign. Outline L hand with R "G."

GROW

L "C" sign in front of body, palm out. Pass R "O" sign up through L "C" spreading fingers as hand emerges.

177

HORSE

R "H" sign with thumb extended. Place on R temple and flap "H" sign down twice.

LEAF

L "1" sign, palm in, tip R. Place R wrist over L index finger and move hand back and forth.

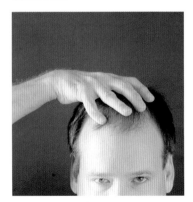

LION

R "C" sign tips down, fingers separated. Place on head and move back.

MONKEY

Scratch sides of the body with both hands, emulating a monkey scratching.

MOON

Form a "C" sign with R thumb and index fingers and place at side of R eye.

MOUSE

Strike tip of nose with R index finger.

PIG

Place back of R hand with fingers together under chin and flap tips down twice.

179

PLANT
R "P" sign passed through and over L "C" sign palm R.

PONY
R "P" sign, place thumb knuckle on R temple, twist finger down twice.

RABBIT

"H" sign both hands, cross at the wrist and wiggle "H" fingers up and down.

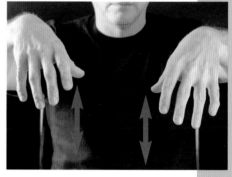

RAIN

"5" sign both hands, palms down, tips out. Move quickly down two or three times.

RAINBOW

R "4" sign, palm in, tips down. Arc L to R indicating a rainbow.

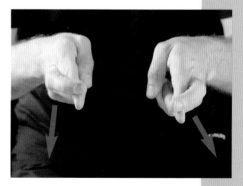

ROAD

"R" sign both hands, palms in, tips out. Move forward.

181

ROOSTER

R "3" sign palm L. Tap forehead twice with thumb.

SHEEP

Place R "V" sign palms up in crook of L forearm, then pretend to clip with the "V" sign.

SKY

R "B" sign palm down placed above and over L side of head, move from L to R ending with fingertips pointing to the sky.

SMOKE

"5" sign both hands, L palm up, tips R. Place tips of R hand in L palm and move up in swirling motion.

SNAKE

Place back of bent R "V" sign under chin and circle forward.

SNOW

"5" sign both hands palms down. Move both hands downward wiggling fingers.

183

STAR

"1" sign both hands, palms out. Repeatedly strike index fingers upwards against each other.

SPIDER

"5" sign both hands palms down, R over with interlocked little fingers. Wiggle all fingers while moving forward.

STREET

"S" sign both hands, palms facing. Move forward.

SUN

Place R "C" sign against side of R eye.

184

TIGER

Claw shape "5" sign, both hands, palms in, tips on cheeks. Move out and repeat.

TREE

R "5" sign palm L. Place R elbow on back of L hand and shake R hand back and forth.

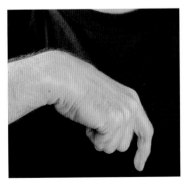

TURKEY

Place back of R "Q" sign on tip of nose, then shake down in front of chest.

185

TURTLE

Place R "A" sign under curved L hand. Extend thumb and wiggle.

WATER

Tap lips twice with index finger of R "W" sign, palm facing L.

WAY

"W" sign both hands palms facing, tips out. Move forward.

THE ART OF SIGN LANGUAGE

186

WEATHER

"W" sign both hands, L palm up tips out, R palm down tips L. Place R on L then reverse.

WIND

"5" sign both hands, palms facing, tips out. Swing back and forth.

WOLF
Tips of R hand around nose then draw away into an "O" sign.

WOODS
R "W" sign, palm L. L "B" sign palm down. Place R elbow on back of L hand and twist back and forth.

YARD
L "B" sign palm down, R "Y" sign palm down. Circle "Y" sign over L hand and forearm.

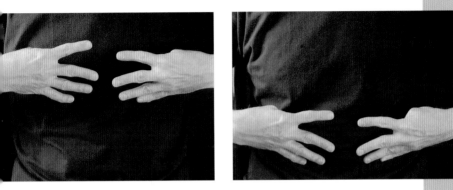

ZEBRA

"F" sign both hands, palms in, tips facing. Place over chest and draw apart. Lower hands and repeat.

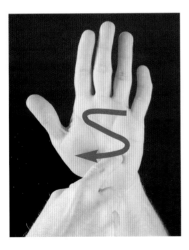

ZOO

L "5" sign palm out. Trace a Z on the L palm with R index finger.

189

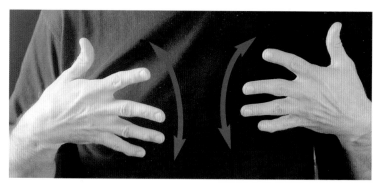

AFRAID

"5" sign both hands, palms in, tips facing. Move up and down several times as if shaking with fear.

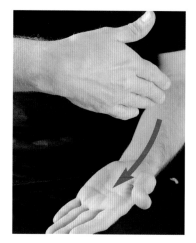

ALL

"B" sign both hands, L palm up, R palm down. Circle L palm with R palm ending with back of R palm resting in L palm.

THE ART OF SIGN LANGUAGE

190

ALONE

"1" sign R hand palm in, tip up. Circle counter-clockwise.

ANGRY

R "5" sign tips clawed on chest, move out in a forceful manner.

descriptions

191

BEAUTIFUL

"5" sign R hand, palm in, tips up. Circle face from R to L ending in an "O" sign, then open fingers palm in, tips up.

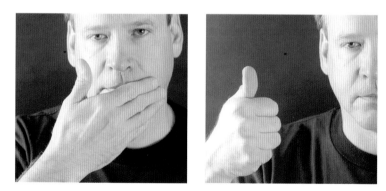

BETTER

R "B" sign, palm in, tips L. Tips on L side of chin then move upward into an "A" sign with thumb extended.

BIG

"B" sign both hands, palms facing, tips out. Move away from each other.

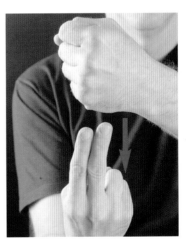

BOTH

R "V" sign palm in, place within a L "C" sign palm in then draw down and out.

CLEAN

L palm up, tips out. R palm down, tips L. Brush R across L as if wiping clean.

COLD

"S" sign both hands knuckles facing. Bring hands close to body and pretend to shiver.

DARK

Palms facing tips up, moving down crossing in front of eyes.

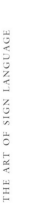

THE ART OF SIGN LANGUAGE

 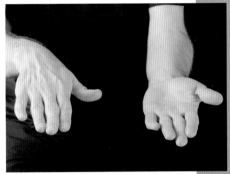

DEAD
R palm down, L hand up in front of the body, then reverse positions.

DIFFERENT
Cross index fingers of both hands, palms out. Pull apart and repeat.

195

DRY

Move bent index finger from L to R across chin.

EASY

Cupped L hand, palm up. Brush up the back of the L fingers twice with the tips of the R palm upwards.

ENOUGH

L "S" sign, knuckles R. Brush R palm over L away from the body.

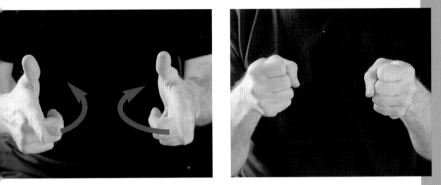

FAST

"L" sign both hands, palms facing, thumbs up. Draw back into "S" signs.

FAT

"5" signs both hands, fingers bent. Bounce off cheeks.

FINE

R "5" sign palms L, place thumb on chest and move slightly outward.

FULL

L "S" sign knuckles R. Brush R palm across L towards body.

FUNNY

Brush tips of nose twice with tips of R "N" sign.

GOOD

Place tips of R hand on the mouth, then move down and place back of R hand on the palm of L hand.

THE ART OF SIGN LANGUAGE

198

GREAT

"G" sign both hands, palms in, tips out. Arc hands apart.

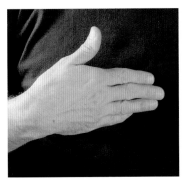

HAPPY

Open R hand, tips left. Brush up chest twice.

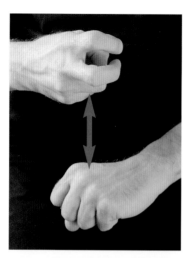

HARD

L "S" sign palms down, hit back of L hand with middle finger of bent R "V" sign and repeat.

HEAVY

Both hands palms up tips out and lower slowly.

HIGH

R "H" sign tips out, palm L. Move up several inches.

THE ART OF SIGN LANGUAGE

200

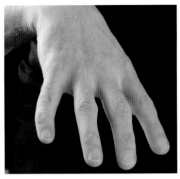

HOT

Place tips of R "5" sign with fingers bent onto the mouth and twist sign down.

HUNGRY

Draw tips of "5" sign with fingers bent down the upper chest.

LARGE

"L" sign palms facing, thumbs up. Move hands apart.

LAZY

R "L" sign palm in. Tap twice just below L shoulder.

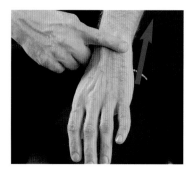

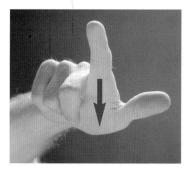

LONG

L "A" sign, knuckles down with arm extended. Run R index finger up L arm.

LOW

R "L" sign palm down, move down.

MANY

"O" sign both hands, palms up. Open into "5" sign palms up.

MORE

"O" sign both hands, palms and tips facing. Tap tips together twice.

NEW

L hand palm up, tips out. Brush back of R hand inward across L palm.

NICE

Place right hand on top of left hand. Slide right hand away from left.

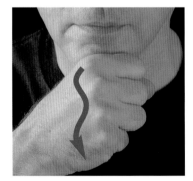

OLD

Place R "S" sign under chin, palm in and move down in a wavy motion.

POOR

Stroke L elbow with R fingers twice.

QUIET

Cross hands at mouth with R index finger on lips. Move apart ending with palms down.

SAD

"5" sign both hands, palms facing and slightly curved. Drop hands to the mouth and then downwards while bending head into an expression of sadness.

205

SAME
"1" sign both hands, palms down, tips out. Bring index fingers together.

SLOW
Draw R palm slowly up back of L palm.

SMALL
Palms facing, thumbs up, tips out. Draw close together.

SMART
Place R index finger on R temple and move out quickly.

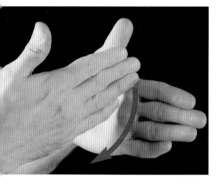

SOME

L hand palm up, R hand palm L tips out. Draw R across L palm.

SOUR

Place R index finger on chin, palm L. Twist so palm faces down.

STRONG

Hold L forearm up, outline shape of L bicep with cupped R hand.

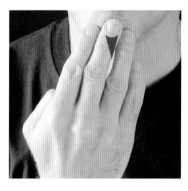

SWEET

R "B" sign, palm in, tips up. Place tips on chin and brush down.

207

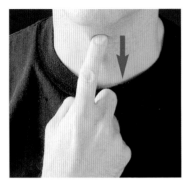

TALL
L hand palm out, tips up. Run R index finger up L palm.

THIRSTY
Draw R index finger down throat.

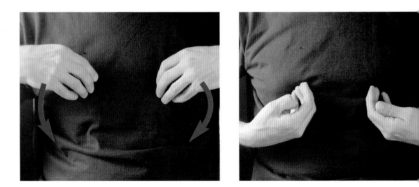

TIRED
Bend both hands palms in and place tips on chest. Turn hands downwards ending with index fingers on chest.

208

TRUE

Place R index finger on mouth then move forward twice.

UGLY

R "X" sign palm down. Draw across nose from L to R.

WARM

Place tips of R "O" sign at mouth then open into a "5" sign.

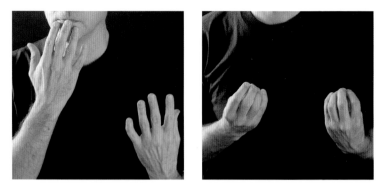

WET

"5" sign both hands. Place R index tip on the mouth then drop both hands into "O" signs.

WRONG

Hit the chin with the knuckles of the R "Y" sign.

THE ART OF SIGN LANGUAGE

210

APPLE

Place knuckles of R index finger into R cheek and twist forward.

BACON

"S" sign both hands, palms down, tips touching. Move away in a wavy motion.

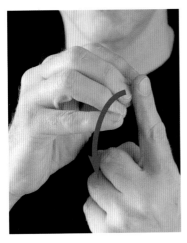

BANANA

Hold up L index finger, mime peeling a banana with tips of R hand.

eating and drinking

211

BOTTLE

Place R "C" sign onto L palm. Lift up into an "S" sign.

 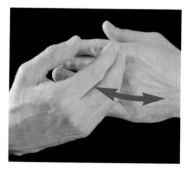

BOWL

Hold cupped hands together palms up, move out and up in shape of a bowl.

BREAD

L hand palm in tips R. Brush back of L hand with little finger side of R hand several times.

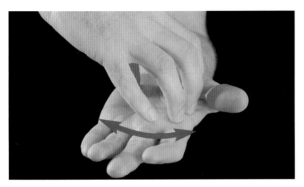

CAKE

Move R "C" sign's fingertips across the palm of L hand.

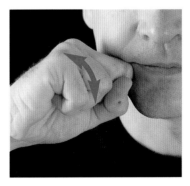

CANDY

Place R index finger just below R side of mouth and twist.

CARROT

Hold R "S" sign up to mouth and twist slightly as if eating a carrot.

213

CHEESE
Twist heels of both palms together.

CHOCOLATE
Place thumb of R "C" sign on back of L hand and circle counter-clockwise.

COFFEE
Place R "S" sign on top of L "S" sign and make a counter-clockwise grinding motion.

THE ART OF SIGN LANGUAGE

214

COOKIE

L hand palm up, tips out. Place tips of R hand on L hand and twist miming cutting out cookies.

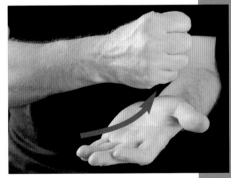

CREAM

L palm up, tips out. Pass R "C" sign over L palm and close into "S" sign as if skimming cream.

215

CUP
Place R "C" sign down on upturned L palm.

DRINK
With R "C" sign hold an imaginary glass and drink.

DINNER
Move fingertips of R hand to mouth, then place R curved hand over flat L hand, palm down. (Signs "eat" and "night").

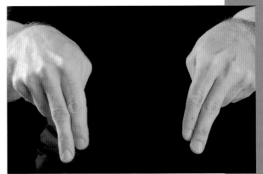

EGG
"H" signs both hands palms in. Hit L "H" sign with R and then draw apart like cracking open an egg.

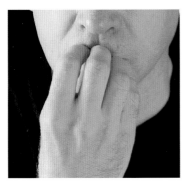
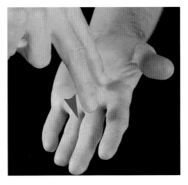

FOOD
Touch mouth with tips of R "O" sign.

FORK
L hand palm up, tips R. Tap L palm with tips of R "V" sign.

FRUIT

Place thumb and index finger of R "F" sign on R cheek, twist turning palm in.

GLASS

L palm up, place R "C" sign onto L palm and raise up indicating a tall glass.

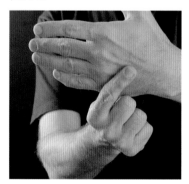

GRAVY

L hand palm in, tips R. R hand "G" sign. Grab bottom of hand with R index and thumb, then slip fingers downward into a closed "G" sign and repeat.

THE ART OF SIGN LANGUAGE

ICE CREAM

Hold a "R" sign at the mouth and move away twice, miming licking an ice cream.

JUICE

Form "J" sign with R hand then raise a "C" sign to the mouth as if drinking.

KNIFE

Strike tips of a R "U" sign against tips of a L index finger and repeat.

LEMON

R "L" sign palm left, thumb in. Tap the chin.

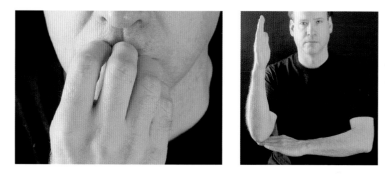

LUNCH

Place the fingertips of the R "O" sign on the mouth several times, then bend the L arm in front of the body pointing R. Place vertical R elbow on L fingertips. (sign "eat" and "noon").

MEAT

L hand palm in, tips R. Move flesh between L thumb and index finger
with R thumb and index finger.

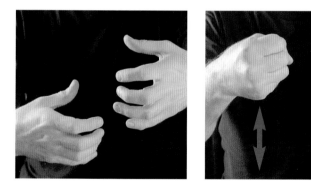

MILK

"S" sign both hands, knuckles in. Mime milking a cow.

ONION

Twist a R "X" sign at the corner of R eye.

ORANGE

R "C" sign, palm L. Squeeze at the mouth into an "S" sign. Repeat motion.

PEA

"1" sign with L hand, palm in, tip R. Tap along finger from along base to tip with R "X" sign.

PEACH

Place tips of R hand on R cheek. Stroke down to the R ending in an "O" sign.

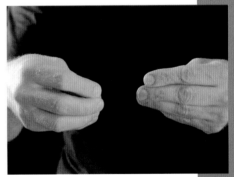

PEAR

L "O" sign palm in, tips R. Stroke L tips with R fingers ending in a R "O" sign.

223

PEPPER
Shake R "O" sign up and down as if sprinkling pepper.

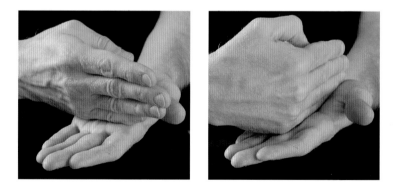

PIE
L hand palm up, tips slightly R. Mime cutting a slice of pie, using the L palm as the tip and the edge of the R palm as the knife.

THE ART OF SIGN LANGUAGE

224

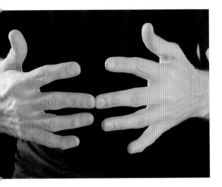

PLATE

"5" sign both hands, palms in, middle fingers touching. Circle backwards ending with palms touching.

POTATO

R "S" sign palm down, pointing R. Tap back of the hand with R "V" sign, fingers bent.

225

PUDDING

L hand palm up, tips out. Place middle finger of R "P" sign in palm then move to the mouth.

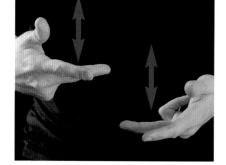 

SALAD

"3" sign both hands, palms up. With fingers curved mime tossing a salad.

SALT

Tap R "V" sign on back of L "V" sign several times.

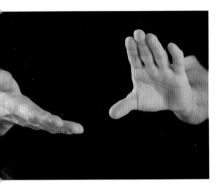

SANDWICH

Both hands palm up, tips out. Slide R hand between thumb and fingers of L hand.

SAUSAGE

"G" sign both hands, tips facing each other, index fingers touching. Draw apart while opening and closing fingers, indicating links of sausage.

SOUP

Place back of R hand into L palm. Move up to mouth as if spooning soup.

SPOON

Scoop a curved R "H" sign into curved L palm and move R hand up to mouth a few times.

STRAWBERRY

R "9" sign, place index finger on the mouth and flick out.

SUGAR

R "H" sign palm in. Stoke fingertips down chin twice.

229

SYRUP

Pass R index finger across lips from L to R.

TEA

Place thumb and index finger of R "F" sign into L "O" sign and stir.

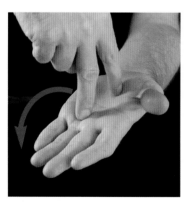

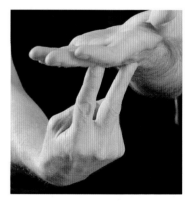

TOAST

Place tips of R "V" sign into L palm. Circle under and touch underside of L hand.

VEGETABLE

R "V" sign. Touch R side of cheek with index finger, twist inward with middle finger ending up on cheek.

WINE

R "W" sign palm L. Circle at R cheek.

ACROSS

L hand palm down, tips R. Slide little finger of R "A" sign palm L across back of L hand.

AIRPLANE

R "Y" sign with index finger extended. Fly through the air like an airplane.

AMBULANCE

R "A" sign, make cross on upper left arm.

on the move

AMERICA

Interlock fingers of both hands and circle in front of the body from R to L.

AROUND

"1" sign both hands, L palm in. Circle R "1"sign around L "1" sign.

BEHIND

"A" sign both hands, knuckles facing, thumbs up. Place hands together and draw R hand back.

233

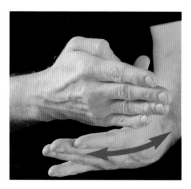

BETWEEN

L hand palm up and tips slanted R.
With R hand palm up tips out, slide
back and forth on the L palm.

BICYCLE

"S" sign both hands, knuckles down.
L hand below R hand. Cycle with
hands.

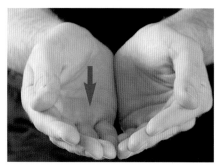

BOAT

Both hands palms up touching together with
little fingers, tips out. Form the shape of a
boat and move forward twice.

BOTTOM

"B" sign both hands palms
down, L tips out, R tips L.
Gently bounce R under L.

BUS
"B" sign both hands palms facing. Mime holding a steering wheel and turning.

CANADA
Grab and shake R side of shirt with R hand.

CAR
"C" sign both hands palms facing, mime turning a steering wheel.

CENT
Circle R index finger in L palm.

235

CHANGE

Place both hands in fists in front of body, with thumbs pointing up. Arc L up and to the right and R down and to the left.

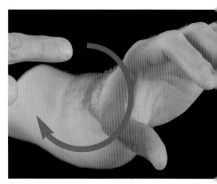

CHURCH

Tap R "C" sign on back of L "S" sign twice.

CIRCLE

L "C" sign. Circle with the R index finger.

COLLEGE
Clap hands together once and circle R hand upward over L.

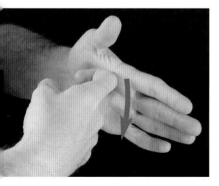 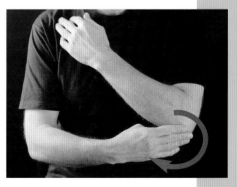

COST
L hand palm R, tips out. Brush R "X" sign down L palm.

COUNTRY
Rub L elbow clockwise with palm of R hand.

237

DIME

Place R index finger on R temple. Drop forward changing into a "10" sign and shake.

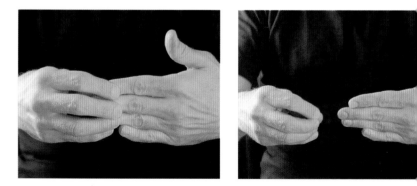

DOLLAR

L hand palm in, tips R. Grab L fingers with R fingers. Move R hand back to R ending in an "O" sign.

238

DOWN
Point index finger down.

DRIVE
"A" sign both hands, move as if turning car's steering wheel.

ENGLAND
Hold L wrist with R hand and move forward and back.

239

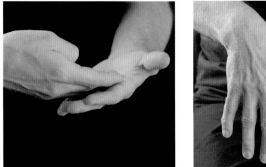

EXPENSIVE

L hand palm up, place back of R "O" sign on L palm, lift out and drop down spreading fingers.

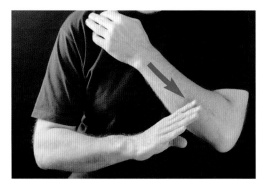

FALL

Slide R hand index finger side down L forearm, which is held in front of the body and at an angle.

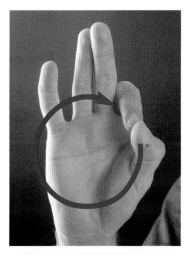

FRIDAY

"F" sign palm out making a small circle in the air.

FROM

"1" sign L hand palm R. Place right "X" sign palm in against L "1" sign and draw back.

241

FRONT

R hand palm in tips L. Drop in front of the face.

HOME

Place tips of R "O" sign on edge of mouth and move to the R cheek.

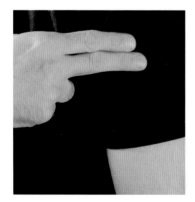

HOSPITAL

R "H" sign, make a cross on L upper arm.

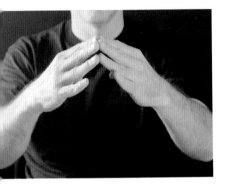

HOUSE

Place tips of both hands together to form a roof, then move apart and down to form sides of house.

LEFT

R "L" sign palm out. Move from R to L.

MONDAY

Circle R "M" sign in the air.

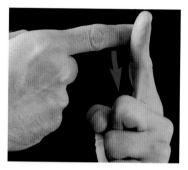

MONEY

L hand palm up, tips out. Tap L palm with back of R "O" sign.

MONTH

"1" sign both hands, L palm R, R palm in tip L. Place R index finger against L index finger and slide down.

MOTORCYCLE

"S" sign both hands held in front of body as if grasping body. Twist inwards twice.

MOVIE

"5" sign both hands, L palm R tips out. R hand palm L tips up. Place palms together and shake R tips back and forth to indicate a flickering motion like a movie.

NICKEL

Tap forehead with middle finger of R "5" sign, then move away.

OFF

Both hands palms down, L tips R and R tips slanted L. Then place R palm on back of L and lift off.

245

ON

Both hands palms down, L tips R and R tips slanted L. Then place R palm on back of L palm.

OVER

Both hands palms down. L hand tips R, R hand tips forward. Pass R over L without touching.

PENNY (Money)

Place R index finger on R temple then move out.

PLACE

"P" sign both hands. Touch tips of middle fingers, circle back towards the body and touch again.

POST OFFICE
Fingerspell "P.O."

QUARTER (Money)
R "L" sign. Place index finger on forehead, move out and flutter last three fingers.

247

RESTAURANT

R "R" sign palm L. Place on R side of mouth and move to L side.

RIGHT

R "R" sign palm L. Move to the R.

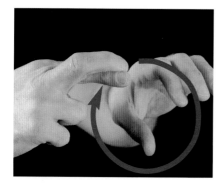

ROUND

L "C" sign, palm and tips out. R "R" sign, palm L. Circle R around L "C" sign.

SATURDAY

R "S" sign palm out. Rotate.

THE ART OF SIGN LANGUAGE

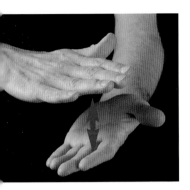

HOOL

m out, tips out. R hand down, tips L.
hands.

SIDE

L hand palm in, tips R. R hand
palm in, tips L. Slide R hand to
R on back of L hand.

SPRING

L "C" sign palm in. Push R "O" sign palm in through L "C" sign opening into a "5"
sign.

STORE

"O" sign both hands, tips down.
Swing out twice.

STRAIGHT

"B" sign both hands, both tips out.
Move R "B" sign straight out across L
"B" sign.

SUMMER

R "X" sign, palm down, knuckles L.
Draw across forehead L to R.

SUNDAY

Both hands palms out. Circle away from
each other.

THE ART OF SIGN LANGUAGE

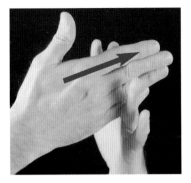

THROUGH

L "5" sign, palm in. R "B" sign palm L. Pass R hand through L middle and 4th fingers.

THURSDAY

Circle R "H" sign, palm in.

sign both hands. Point R index fin-
at L index finger and touch.

TOP

"B" sign both hands, L palm R, tips up. R palm down, tips L. Rest R palm on L tips.

251

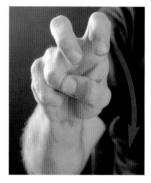

TRAIN

"H" sign both hands, palms down. L tips out, R tips L. Rub R "H" back and forth on L "H."

TRIP

R "V" sign. Bend fingers and move forward in circular motion.

TRUCK

"T" sign both hands, palms facing. Mime holding and moving a steering wheel.

TUESDAY

Circle R "T" sign, palm out.

252

NDER
and palm down, tips R. R "A"
ı, thumb up palm L. Pass under L
ı.

UNTIL
"1" sign both hands. Arc tip of R index
over to the left.

UP
Point index finger up.

WEDNESDAY
Circle R "W" palm out.

253

WINTER

"W" sign both hands, palms facing, tips out. Press arms against body and shake hands back and forth in shivering motion.

WHEEL

R "W" sign, palm L, tips out. Rotate.

WORLD

"W" sign both hands, tips out. Place R "W" on top of L, then circle R "W" around L and return to original position.

THE ART OF SIGN LANGUAGE

255